SILENT BOB SPEAKS

Silent Bob Speaks

The Collected Writings of Kevin Smith

TITAN BOOKS

The publisher & author would like to thank the following
publications for permission to reprint material:

Arena Magazine

Details

New Jersey Monthly

Film Comment

Silent Bob Speaks: The Collected Writings of Kevin Smith

ISBN: 1 84576 080 8

Published by Titan Books

A division of Titan Publishing Group Ltd, 144 Southwark St, London, SE1 0UP

First edition May 2005

10 9 8 7 6 5 4 3 2

Published by arrangement with Miramax. Cover Design by Miramax Books.

Did you enjoy this book? We love to hear from our readers. Please e-mail us at:

readerfeedback@titanemail.com

Visit our website: **www.titanbooks.com**

A CIP catalogue record for this title is available from the British Library.

Printed and bound in the UK by Cox & Wyman Ltd.

PART TWO.

PART THREE.

PART FOUR.

Contents

A^S WITH MOST THINGS IN LIFE, this book's secret origin is tied directly to gonzo documentarian and would-be president-unseater Michael Moore.

It was late 1995 when I met Mike, through our mutual friend John Pierson—the indie guru responsible for a far better book than this: *Spike, Mike, Slackers & Dykes: A Guided Tour Across a Decade of American Independent Cinema* (recently updated and rereleased as *Spike Mike Reloaded).* Back when John was a producer's rep, he used to shepherd indie films into the distribution corrals of mini-majors (like Miramax, or Island Pictures) and maxi-majors (like Warner Bros.) by acting as a sort of agent/cheerleader for such nascent filmmakers as Spike Lee (with his sexy debut effort, *She's Gotta Have It),* Michael Moore (and his first shot across the conservative brow, *Roger & Me),* and hacky ol' me (with my amateur hour DIY-er, *Clerks).*

The night John introduced us, both Mike and I were nursing a big, bad case of the sophomore blues. After making splashes with our first films and being lauded with awards and enough high praise to convince us we could do no wrong, Mike and I, separately, signed on with Universal's and Polygram's joint indie arm experiment Gramercy to make our follow-up features. A pair of scrappy, tubby iconoclasts (at least, that's what we were dubbed) infiltrating Universal's legendary, lot-based Black Tower and working (sort of) within the studio system? What havoc would they wreak? What bold, anti-establishment statements would they strong-arm the corporate whores they duped into giving them millions of dollars into releasing?

I made *Mallrats.* Mike made *Canadian Bacon.*

I'm not sure, but I think the theatrical releases of our films were two of the worst in Gramercy's short history. In fact, we probably contributed to the motherfucker's downfall. Theatrically, the six-million-dollar *Mallrats* trapped only $2.1 million at the box office, while the eleven-million-dollar-budgeted *Bacon* fried up merely $163,971.00. And as if that wasn't bad enough, the reviews were vicious. The love letters we'd received for our first films became bitter, angry breakup notes from critics who, in the span of one film, went from believing in us to chasing us out of the village with torches and pitchforks. We went from indie darlings to indie cautionary tales: "This is what happens when you give these people a budget," they said, derisively. The future looked bleak.

It was about all this and Moore that Michael and I commiserated the night Pierson introduced us. But that night, Pierson was affording us an opportunity to forget we were veterans of the Gramercy war who'd returned to our country only to be spat on and chided as baby-killers; that night, we were gathered to do a book reading of *Spike, Mike* at the new Barnes & Noble bookstore in Union Square. But as the limo pulled up to the multistory affair (situated mere yards from where I'd dormed only a few years earlier, back when I unsuccessfully tried to start a college career at the New School for Social Reasearch), Mike could think of little else but how badly his flick had done. I wouldn't be exaggerating by describing him as depressed, even. Me? I'd already dealt with my *Rats* grief; but then, I was never the serious, issue-chasing documentarian Mike was. *Rats* was merely a lesser version of *Clerks* (indeed, it was pitched as *Clerks* Redux). Mike had risked his rep as a corporate lion-tamer and gotten spanked for helming a fictional fancy about an unpopular president who starts a war with another country to boost his Q rating (which, I think, has a lot to do with Mike's current Bush-hunt; if he can clothes-hanger the warmonger out of the White House, not only can he sort of prove that Bush lied about Iraq and earn America a chance to right our currently abysmal reputation amongst the international community, but more importantly, he gets to say "See? *Canadian Bacon* was a prognostication of things to come that was way ahead of its time!" When all's said and done, all filmmakers care about is being right).

Mike was wearing his *Bacon* stains on his face, that night: he'd let an unkempt version of his now everpresent beard grow in, almost as if saying to the world

"Fuck it. You won." As we were ushered up to the second floor of Barnes & Noble, he was hardly recognizable to what turned out to be a sizeable crowd of mostly Mike admirers, all of whom'd been rabid, collegiate *TV Nation* fans. When the hangdog once-and-future king finally noticed the smiling throng, he looked to me and Pierson, offering surprisedly, "Wow—this many people turned out for a book reading?"

All three of us (and Tommy Hicks, the male lead of *She's Gotta Have It)* sat before a crowd of about a hundred as John read passages from his book that related to the films we'd been involved in. Following the reading, the floor was opened to questions from the crowd. And this is where I witnessed the miracle.

Mike was asked a question—a *TV Nation* question, I believe, but the question wasn't important. What *was* important was Mike's *answer:* it yielded a wave of laughter from all assembled. As I'm sure most of you know, Mike can be a pretty funny guy. However, due to the financial and critical drubbing that *Canadian Bacon* had taken, Mike had forgotten that. Hearing a bunch of people—*real* people, not just Monday morn-

ing figures on a box office spreadsheet—validate his
unique point of view reawakened the sleeping giant.

And just like that, Michael Moore was reborn.

I've never watched a human being inflate before.
Deflate, sure—I deflate every time the wife says "Your
dick's not small, babe; it's just the right size." But
inflate? That's a rarity. Mike went from the broken man
I chatted up during the limo ride to the event to a man
with a mission: a comeback mission. As the evening
continued, and Mike's responses got more and more
laughs from the crowd, two words danced across his
eyes: "I'm back."

On the limo ride from the bookstore, Mike interro-
gated John about his book deal: which publishers he
shopped the book around to, how long he took to write
it, etc. Mike was suddenly on fire. At one point, when I
jokingly chided him for being a common-man cru-
sader who was being driven around in the back of a
limo, he rolled down his window and, with tongue
firmly planted in cheek, yelled out at the folks we
passed, "I'M MICHAEL MOORE! MAN OF THE PEOPLE!"
By the time we dropped him off at his place, the man of

the people was just flat-out giddy. And while I assumed
it was just the high one gets from making a crowd
laugh, in retrospect, it was really the high one cruises
on the moment they figure out the rest of their lives.

A year or so later, Mike released *Downsize This*. It
sold millions of copies. He was, indeed, back.

(While I never read *Downsize*, I *did* check out the
dedication page, to see if he gave Pierson props for the
book idea—because without the confluence of events
surrounding John's book reading, I doubt Mike
would've arrived at the same conclusion that started
the chain of events which eventually led to *Fahrenheit
9/11*. Alas, there was no shout-out to Pierson in the
dedication. I guess Mike saw the situation differently
than I did. Regardless, consider this that long overdue
shout-out.)

Cut to years later. I'd been writing a monthly column for the British magazine *Arena*. One of my
columns was about morbid obesity and being prescribed a fat-blocker that gave me greasy shits. It was
off of that piece that I received the following call . . .

"Hold for Harvey Weinstein."

"Holding."

"Kevin?"

"Am I in trouble for something?"

"I just read the piece you wrote for *Arena* magazine—about the greasy shit pills."

"Yeah?"

"It's great."

"Thanks, Boss."

"How long have you been doing them?"

"About two months now. The bitch is that you can't
really fart anymore without worrying you're gonna
blow grease into your underwear."

"I meant how long have you been writing the
columns."

"Oh. I think I've written five or six so far."

"Why don't you write a book for Miramax Books?"

"I don't know, Boss. I'm not really a book kinda guy.
I just write essays."

"Well write a book full of essays, then. Have you
seen how many copies *Stupid White Men* has sold?"

"Yeah, but I'm not political. I just like writing about
shit that happens to me. Or greasy shit."

"Well do that and we'll collect 'em all into a book. You can be *our* Michael Moore."

See how it came full circle–like?

That was two years ago. Now, as this book hits the shelves, thanks to the insanely (financially) successful *Fahrenheit 9/11*, Harvey has Michael Moore *himself* as his Michael Moore. And you have the book about my greasy shits.

I hate to tell ya, but I'm afraid Harvey made out better than you, folks.

I'VE GOTTA THANK A FEW FOLKS, without whom this collection wouldn't exist.

First off, Anthony Noguera, the mad genius at *Arena* who thought I'd make a halfway decent contributor to his mag. He's suffered many long hours, waiting for last-minute copy that I should've turned in weeks prior, yet didn't say "Oh, fuck that deadline-breaking fat fuck…" when Miramax Books asked if they could republish my articles.

Gabe Soria and Joe Doughrity, from the dot-com

casualty psycomic.com, let me run rampant with a column called "Developing the Monkey" which I wrote during preproduction on *Jay and Silent Bob Strike Back.* Thanks, guys, for affording me the opportunity to use the other side of my brain when I was directing a movie in which half the dialogue was "Snoogans!" and "BUNNNGGGG!!!"

David Keeps and *Details* version 1.0, who let me write about strippers who wouldn't date me and my favorite non-Kev subject, *Degrassi.*

Me and Chris Ryall, over at moviepoopshoot.com—the site I own—for letting me hype the little movie that couldn't, *Jersey Girl.*

Harvey Weinstein, who thought—even for a moment—that I could do Mike Moore–type business with this book, bless his deluded li'l heart. As always, Boss, I appreciate the unfounded vote of confidence.

Gail Stanley, who reminded me daily to finish this intro.

Ms. Catanzarite, my fifth grade teacher, who encouraged me to write.

Donald, my brother, who was the first person who

ever read one of my dopey little essays and laughed—with, not at—thus providing the encouragement that's fueled me for the past twenty-five years.

Mom and Dad, who bought me this big ol' monstrosity that Smith Corona put out in the early '90's that basically converted an electric typewriter into a primitive (yet functional) word processor. I spent many a high school night not getting pussy banging away on those keys, writing stories about . . . well, *getting* pussy.

Jenny, who gives me the pussy, and without whom there's no point in doing anything—pussy-related or otherwise.

And finally, to Kristin Powers—my long, long suffering editor on this book, who's waited patiently for two years to finish something for which all of the contents were pretty much already in existence. Never have an editor's best efforts been so stymied by one man's inability to focus on more than one thing at a time—and all for a book that probably won't move more than ten copies. My bad, Kristin. Feel free to change the title from *Silent Bob Speaks* to *Fahrenheit 9/11* if you think it'll help.

PART ONE

Introductions Suck

Let's assume you all know me, and I know all of you (all eight of you reading this, that is), and move forward with the dish and deets.

What follows is all a blurry haze of weird, unnatural sex, dangerous nonprescription drugs, and far too much discussion about the impending Screen Actors Guild strike. I can't be held accountable for how factual my take on the proceedings is going to be. All I can say is that, over the next twenty-five weeks here at Psycomic.com, I'll *try* to be honest (which is more than most 'net columnists will give you).

Last week, my life became a thrill-a-minute joyride through the glamorous and exciting world of making motion pictures, and I figure that'd probably be more

interesting to share with you guys and gals than a
weekly dissertation on what comics I like and why, or
who I think is fucking up the comics industry, or
whether Hal or Kyle is the one, true Green Lantern. We
pretty much all know the answers to those questions
(*Green Arrow* because I'm writing it, anyone who thinks
the kids will *ever* come back to this medium, and Hal
Jordan), so there's little point in talking about it. This
shit that I'm about to tell you, however, is real inside
dope, and I need you to promise you're not going to
share it with anyone else, as I need my day job, and I
don't want to get kicked out of the movie club for talking smack about the secret process of how Hollywood
works (to kill the suspense: it doesn't).

We started what is referred to in the movie biz as
"preproduction"—which essentially means everything
that has to happen before Jason Mewes can utter the
immortal line "Snoogans!" on film. The script's been
written (and rewritten, and rewritten), the studio (the
Dimension arm of Miramax) is humoring us enough to
break off a couple bones to finance the realization of it,
and all that's left to do (aside from the thousand boring-

ass technical details that the producers take care of while I'm sleeping or watching TV) is cast some open roles. What better way to forge the single step that'll mark the start of this million-mile debacle-in-the-making than by planting one's foot firmly in (hel)L.A.? If you're casting, it's the place to be—as it's the town where all the actors and actresses seem to migrate and sleep with one another.

To wit, here was how week one and that process played out.

SUNDAY

Contrary to popular belief, I don't mind getting out of "the Jers" every now and then. It's not so much that I hate the state (the *wife* does—with a vengeance), as that it's nice to break with the domestic routine from time to time. To appreciate this, you have to understand my average day consists of an early rise to the tune of a yowling child (who wants neither love from me nor her mother, but instead to be placed in front of the tube for more predawn *Teletubbies* hate-marches), the massive consumption of at *least* a boxful of what-ever presweetened cereal I found a triple coupon for that week, many failed attempts to get into my wife's drawers, and finally, a nod-out at around eight P.M., while bitterly watching a DVD of some flick that made more money than all of mine put together at the box office. From cradle to grave, if I'm lucky, all my days will resemble that schedule.

But not last week. I packed up kit and kin and flew to Bev-er-ly. Because I'm a superstitious weenie, I insist that the wife and I fly out first, with the baby and her grandparents following the next day (as we're going to be gone for over a week, and she doesn't know how to operate the stove just yet because she's fifteen months old, we didn't want to leave the kid at home; and as she's a handful, and I'm going to be as useless as tits on a fire hydrant because I'm working out there, the wife's parents graciously opted to tag along and help out). We get to L.A. Sunday afternoon, and *one* of us is in Heaven.

See, the wife's originally from the City of the Angels. Well, really, she's originally from Boca Raton, but had been living in L.A. for seven years and working at *USA*

Today writing features about the Vapid and Vacant when I met her (I was one of the V&Vs in question, and our meet-cute story is just about as adorable as two bunny rabbits fucking, but I'll save that for another time when I'm running late on a column deadline; like today). So for her, it's always a sort of homecoming when we go to L.A.—especially since it's getting "really cold" for her in Jersey (it's about sixty-five, mind you).

Me? Fuck, I hate Los Angeles. The reasons for which are pretty routine and boring enough to fashion a sitcom out of, so I'll not regale you with the fine print, and leave it simply at me and the town don't really get along, is all.

We get to the Four Seasons hotel, judge it goodly enough to sleep in without fear of being chewed apart at night by cockroaches (my secret hotel paranoia), hurl our bags into a corner of the room, and rush out to catch a moving picture. As we are in a major metropolitan area, there are certain cultural outlets (yes—the irony of L.A. and the phrase "cultural outlets" is not lost on me) that one must take advantage of because one doesn't find such in the sticks of the Jersey 'burbs. That night, we opt to take in an art house picture that wouldn't make it to our neck of the woods for, oh, say two years. *Girl Fight* is on the menu that eve, and it's a tough sit for me because I've seen it already, in Sundance, when I was a judge there last January (Hey everyone! Look at me! I'm pretty fucking full of myself and important!). But the wife hasn't peeped it yet, so I suffer through another screening, even though it's the kind of film you really only need to see once (which, to my mind, is a ringing endorsement, as most flicks don't warrant seeing ever; especially my own).

We turn in after that, as tomorrow starts the long process of meet-and-greets.

Kevin Smith is a filmmaker, the author of the Funk and Wagnalls dictionary, a comic book writer, a student of the Cobra Kai school of karate, the proprietor of a comic book shop, a jet fighter pilot, a husband, a father, and an all-around ace character.

Monday

WE'RE IN L.A. to cast some roles in the new flick
we're doing, the working title of which is *VA5*,
which stands for *View Askew 5*, which stands for
"We're not giving away the title just yet." Why we've
shrouded the production in a Lucasian level of secrecy
is beyond me, as A) most folks don't give a shit *what*
we're making next, and B) most folks immediately—
and rightly—assume it's another one of those pictures
with the long-haired vulgar kid and the fat guy who
never says anything. It's an accurate description, but
one that leaves out the crucial bit of data that it's the
last of those flicks, as it's time to close the book on the
"Jersey Trilogy" (which has overstayed its welcome by
a chapter; some say four), and move on to more adult

fare (like hardcore, triple-penetration porn—the jewel
in the crown of any filmmaker worth his or her salt).

   In order to cast a picture (or rather, *this* picture),
my producer Scott Mosier and I sit down with a series
of actors and actresses we've either never met or never
heard of, looking for someone who can fit snugly into
our two-dimensional/one-note little programmer.
These are called "meet-and-greets" as that's chiefly all
you do: meet the actor/actress (as they're meeting
you), and greet them with a string of bullshit about
how this is going to be the most important role they
could ever play (as they greet you with a web of lies
about how they're up to the challenge). It's a fairly
innocuous process, and easy on the eyes, as you're
meeting a slew of the Best-looking People in the World.
In fact, were one not so secure with himself, it'd be
more like a meet-and-*weep*—as you'd lay eyes on these
gods-cut-from-stone, and recall that you yourself are a
tub of lard from the Jersey shore who could never get
beyond his fascination with Devil Dogs, and, as such,
neglected the opportunity to exercise or take daily
showers. Thankfully, I've long since accepted my place

in the Universe, and have put the gut to work for me as the quiet and husky half of the Jay-and-Silent-Bob Equation—which is kinda like the Anti-life Equation, but there's no Mobius Chair (that's for the comics folks who're still reading; see? I threw you a bone).

As mentioned previously, we're meeting some actresses and actors you haven't heard of (yet), so rather than drop names that still fly under your radar, I'll mention only the cats you're familiar with (or have jerked and rubbed off to in the lonely quiet of your bedrooms at night). Mind you—not every cat doesn't wind up in the picture because they're not good enough; in fact, some cats, though I dig them immensely, I reject out of hand because I respect them too much, and this picture will be no feather in their caps.

Which brings up a really salient point about these meetings. Nobody knows what picture we're making next. We've not made the script public yet—not even to the casting folks or agents responsible for bringing in the talent we're meeting. Now, most take a look at the trajectory of our career and see two crude comedies at the start; one that clicks (*Clerks*), and one that doesn't quite click, or rather, simply flops (*Mallrats*). After that, we do a critically hailed picture about relationships (*Chasing Amy*), and another critically hailed picture about religion and faith (*Dogma*). Mind you, both the latter flicks are crude comedies as well, but since they also take a moment to address some important (to someone) issues, they're somehow considered more respectable (not *my* logic, mind you; this is what the newspaper and magazine critics tell me). So someone who handles talent (an agent, though that definition is questionable as all hell) looks at our previous stuff, hears we're making a new movie, and assumes that we're fashioning another funny-but-issue-laden indie picture like the last two.

Not fucking so. Not fucking so in the least.

This time around, we're making a flat-out, no-socially-redeeming-value, made-or-broken-by-the-opening-weekend comedy. There will be no lesbians (unless they're played strictly for laughs) and even less talk about the Lord, Jesus Christ (unless He weighs in on the SAG strike); just hijinks and antics the like of which you haven't seen since *Mallrats* (which was *barely* seen, so all our rehashing of the same material may actually wind up seeming fresh).

This is what's called a "step backward." Making a balls-to-the-wall comedy at this point in our careers isn't even a lateral move, really. A lateral move would be a thoughtful, satiric, talky piece about Mormons or some other religious group. No, to mine territory that we've mined before—and rather financially unsuccessfully, I might add—is considered a step backward. When the picture comes out (hell—*if* the picture comes out), the critics who've watched our careers with interest, or were simply forced to review our shit by virtue of their day jobs, will probably say "Smith should be beyond this kind of nonsense by now, but apparently decided to take another weak stab at it. Thumbs-down." Knowing this in advance, you may ask yourself why we're bothering then.

Before we get there, I want to clear up a fine point. When I say "we" I'm not using the royal "we" or anything. When I say "we" I mean me and the usual gang of idiots who've charged into the breach with me before (Scooter; Laura Greenlee, our line producer;

Ratface, our production designer; Mewes, our jour-
neyman stoner; Affleck, our only famous friend, etc.—
the people I've been through this with more than
once). And while I may be the guy who scribbles down
the naughty words and makes sure the actors pro-
nounce them on camera properly, no writer/director
is an island. Film is a very collaborative medium. *I*
never make movies. *We* make movies.

And all that nobility aside—at the end of the day,
isn't it best to spread the blame around in advance,
just in case the picture is absolute dogshit? I think so.

Kevin Smith has made a few movies and written a
few comics—both with too many words in them. He
won a Harvey Award once, but the Eisners have thus
far ignored him (probably with good reason). When
he's not spouting off at Psycomic, he's spouting off at
his website, the View Askewniverse. But before all else,
he's a husband and a father (yes—he's gotten laid at
least once).

Still Monday

SO WHY ARE WE BOTHERING with *VA5* if we're cocksure the critics are going to not only turn their backs on us, but do so after having served up our entrails with pithy dismissals and half stars galore? It's quite simple, really.

We should be able to make any movie we want, stupid or not—so long as it doesn't cost too much, and is reasonably guaranteed to make its money back for our distributor. That, for the curious, is why we're allowed to keep making movies. Some cats (particularly the denizens of Internet movie chat boards) can't figure out why we're allowed to continue lensing flicks, when we never seem to grow as visual storytellers, or keep making—what's to them—the same movie. The answer is that we've never lost anybody money.

I'll say that again: we've never lost anybody money. Granted, we came close with *Rats*; but even that made a killing on video and, more recently, DVD. And even though we've never had a breakout, blockbuster, monstro-hit (our highest-grossing effort was thirty-one million bucks), we've never spent much money making those pictures (said flick only cost ten million bucks), so the return per investment usually pleases the suits (we earned three times what we spent; and that was just the theatrical release). If you can make some cats a little green without losing them any in the process, they'll let you shoot, shoot, shoot, like you're Oswald in the Book Depository.

It doesn't always work like that for some filmmakers. Some cats let their budgets escalate with every successive movie they make until they get to the point where it's tough to turn a profit, because their pictures cost a hundred-plus million bucks. But while I'm a glutton at a $1.99 buffet, I'm incredibly responsible when it comes to spending other people's money. I don't need bigger budgets, because I make movies in which people talk at each other for an hour and a half, and shooting talk is cheap. Shooting *explosions* is expensive, so I tend to shy away from those, particularly because explosions have no place in a conversation about autofellatio or the like.

So, because I work cheap and always turn a profit, I get to make whatever flick I want with my gaggle of friends. This time, it's a dumb comedy—partly because we all thought the script was funny (well, Affleck and Mewes did, anyway), and partly because the last time we made a picture, we got all manner of hate mail and a couple of death threats. It wasn't a good time for most, to work their asses off on what they felt was an entertaining-yet-thoughtful potboiler about faith and spirituality, only to have so-called Christians let us know that the Son of God had charged them with smiting us for our efforts. After dealing with that for two years, it just felt like it was time to do something light and airy, for which the only death threats we may receive won't be related to some jihad, but instead to the quality of the flick itself (i.e., "Your movie sucked so hard, I want to kill you."). And while the people who tend to intellectualize a medium as silly as motion pictures maintain that *Amy* and *Dogma* are high-water marks in our careers, you wouldn't believe the number of people who'll come up to me and say "*Mallrats* is the bomb, yo. You should make another one of those." Granted, they may be twelve, but I'm no snob; a fan of my work is a fan of my work, regardless of whether he or she has sprouted pubes yet.

That being said, all these actors and actresses we're meeting with are under the impression we're doing what we like to call a "classy picture." Since we're not, and we know we're not but they don't, the meet-and-greets we're able to line up are really impressive. If some of these folks had any clue they were meeting on a flick that features a monkey in a prominent role, they might've held out for a meeting with a more visionary director. As they have no clue what the script's about, they deign to meet with me and Scooter.

One such cat who probably would've taken the meeting regardless of his foreknowledge of the flick's contents was Jay Mohr. You may know him as Bob

Sugar, the asshole agent who backstabs the title character in the sublime *Jerry Maguire*. Or you may know him as the lead in the short-lived yet on-the-money Fox series *Action* (or, if you're an Opie and Anthony nut, you might recognize his name from his many appearances on their radio broadcast). Whatever you know him from, you don't know him unless you've spent some time with him in real life. He's a really, really funny motherfucker, with a head screwed so straight on his shoulders that you're amazed he's able to navigate the waters of show business. He summed up meet-and-greets best when he broke them down to me and Scooter thusly: "You know and like my stuff, I know and like your stuff. We know this because we say 'no' to having lots of these meetings. But when we actually hook up for one, we don't really mention the mutual appreciation, because it's assumed. We really want to meet just to make sure we're not assholes."

While Mohr may not be right for the flick we're doing now, I will eventually find something to do with Mohr. Because life's too short to *not* work with a guy that smart.

Kevin Smith has made a few movies and written a few comics—both with too many words in them. He won a Harvey Award once, but the Eisners have thus far ignored him (probably with good reason). When he's not spouting off at Psycomic, he's spouting off at his website, the View Askewniverse. But before all else, he's a husband and a father (yes—he's gotten laid at least once).

Still Fucking Monday, and Finally Tuesday

PRIOR TO MOHR, the first person we met with that Monday morning, courtesy of our casting maven, Christine Sheaks, was Judd Nelson. This was a cool meeting, as Judd was in the then-and-still-classic *The Breakfast Club*. Aside from that, I'm also a big softie for a little picture called *From the Hip*, which was directed by *Porky's* helmer Bob Clark and written by a then un-*Ally*ed David E. Kelley. If you've never seen it, try digging it up at a video store, especially if you love courtroom flicks like I do.

We talk about those flicks, as well as the myriad other flicks he's done, and the whole time I'm thinking to myself "I must get this guy into the flick, somewhere. He is *so* the fucking man." This is, after all, the genius who put the perfect inflection on the line "Hey, Cherry—do *you* belong to the Physics Club?" Judd snaps me out of my daze by thanking me for the shout-out I gave him in *Dogma*—a line I'd completely forgotten about prior to that. It's a mutual lovefest.

After Judd and Jay Mohr, we sit down with Shannon Elizabeth—she of *American Pie* and *Scary Movie* fame. She's the big surprise of the day, as she's smart, self-aware, and incredibly lacking in pretense. While going into the meeting, she wasn't on our radar. We knew her simply as the *American Pie* and *Scary Movie* girl. But in the meeting, the worm turns. She gives such great meeting that she's the *only* person on our radar at that point. She's also honest as hell, and dishes up some good gossip, which is a big plus with a catty old lady like me. And since these meetings are more about checking out an actor's personality than their acting abilities, you really want to connect with them on a personal level because, remember, you have to spend two to three months with this person when you commit to them. Their performance in character will come eventually; it's their off-screen persona that you'll never be able to mold. So you *want* someone on set you can bullshit with and like when you call "cut." Because you say "cut" a lot when you're directing.

So Jay Mohr, Judd Nelson, and Shannon Elizabeth were the standouts of Monday. Scooter and I talk about them that night, when we meet with Laura Greenlee (our line producer) and Jon Gordon (our Miramax production exec and godfather) to discuss Austin, Texas vs. Los Angeles, California, and which is better to shoot in. True—most of my shit takes place in Jersey. But Jersey's not the cheapest state to shoot in, and since this is a road picture that only *starts* in Jersey, there's a need to find a state that can double for the rest of the country (and I hate to admit it, but Red Bank doesn't look like Colorado).

During this meeting, the crucial issue of what to name the production company comes up. Our production company is called View Askew. However, when you make a flick, you need to do it under the aegis of *another* production company, so if anything goes

wrong, your production company doesn't get the pants
sued off it (I know—why bother having a production
company in the first place, if you're just constantly
changing the name while in production? My best guess
is for the stationery).

On *Clerks* we had no production company name
other than View Askew (we didn't know any better). On
Mallrats, we called the company "Unstable Molecules"
in honor of Stan Lee, who did a cameo for the picture.
Chasing Amy was shot under "Too Askew," *Dogma* was
under "Plenary Indulgence," and the short-lived *Clerks*
cartoon was done under "Toon Askew." What to go with
this time?

Laura throws out the brilliant suggestion that wins
the title after we talk about how this is the last of the
Jersey flicks with Jay and Bob. She suggests "Askews
Me"—you know, because we're leaving. Get it? It's so
clever that, as far as I'm concerned, Laura doesn't have
to work another day on the picture. She's earned her
salary with that one suggestion.

TUESDAY

Tuesday morning, Sheaks tells us that we're going to meet-and-greet with Kate Hudson (she of *Almost Famous* fame) in New York City when we head home the following week. I say that's cool, but I'm really interested in meeting with Amy Smart, too (she of *Road Trip* and *Outside Providence* fame). There's a pretty big part for a girl in the flick, and usually we'd just cast one of the actresses we've worked with before (we work with a lot of the same people in our flicks). But this time, we want to go with one we've never worked with before, based on the nature of the story.

That's about the extent of our casting activities that day, as we spend the rest of Tuesday recording the commentary tracks for the *Clerks* cartoon DVD (due out in January). I'm jawing on it, of course, as is Scooter, Dave Mandel (the guy we created the cartoon with), Chris Bailey (the guy who designed the cartoon), Jason Mewes (he of "Jay" fame), Jeff Anderson ("Randal" to the fans), and Brian O'Halloran ("Dante," natch). Jay, Jeff, and Brian are all in the movie, and we've met with them before, so there's no reason to meet-and-greet them. They know all our bullshit, and we know all theirs.

Jeff's going through his own bit of meet-and-greets, however, as he's getting ready to direct his first film. It's from a script he wrote, and he's promised me a bit part. Hopefully, I don't play *too* big an asshole (I've already got that covered, just fine, in real life).

Later that night, Scooter and I meet with Laura and Jon again to pore over pictures of possible locations in Austin. The locations person out there goes to a place, takes a bunch of pics, then tapes them together in standard manila folders, and ships them off to us. This place looks like a medical lab. Great. That place looks like a diamond exchange. Perfect. When we're done with the pics, we talk further about Austin vs. L.A., and let them both know that there's a Kate Hudson meeting set up for next week, and we're still working on tracking down Amy Smart.

After that, Jen and I take Scooter, Mandel, Jeff, Brian, Paul Dini (he of *Batman Animated* fame), Dan Etheridge (a good friend of ours who's also a producer), and Jen's friend Lisa out to dinner at a place called the

Ivy that makes this gumbo you'd step on your own mother's neck to get at. Everyone talks about movies, the impending strike, and *Batman Beyond: The Return of the Joker* (which Paul's involved in, of course; see? more bones for the comics-only people). The bill comes, and with tip, it's about a seven-hundred-fifty-dollar meal (only because I'm such a sap, and can't *not* tip fifty percent on a restaurant check—even when the service is shitty, which it wasn't at the Ivy). I suddenly miss how affordable the Broadway Diner in Red Bank is. The same crew of people eating would probably cost about a hundred and fifty, with tip.

But then, the Diner doesn't have that awesome gumbo.

Kevin Smith actually gets paid for this shit. He'd like to note that while he has a mother, he never stepped on a crack and broke her back, and also that he has a baby, though her head never popped off. He's since come to believe that everything he was told as a child was a lie.

Wednesday

SHEAKS (SHE WHO IS IN CHARGE OF CASTING) comes to the hotel in the morning and shows Scooter and me tape of actresses who I'm not familiar with. Jen elects to sit in, as she feels it sounds fun. After an hour, she changes her tune. Watching tape of actors and actresses can be pretty painful if you have no vested interest in who gets cast.

Most actors have what's called a "reel," a tape of what they feel are the shining moments of their career; a greatest hits affair, as it were. The actors and actresses who've hit it big don't rely on reels because they rightly assume people must know who they are by now. For example, Heather Graham needs no reel; after her stints as Rollergirl in *Boogie Nights,* and as the spy who shags Austin Powers in *Austin Powers: The Spy Who Shagged Me,* most cats on both sides of the movie screen know who she is.

Heather Graham is who Dimension would like us to cast opposite Jay in *VA5.* I don't have any objections to this (I've been a fan of hers since *Drugstore Cowboy*), but I'd like to meet her before offering the role. For all I know, Heather hates the flicks we've done, and has sworn never to work with us. The last thing I want to do is offer a non-fan a major role in one of our flicks, and have that actor or actress gather their friends in a drunken, derisive reading of the script, during which people are cackling and offering up such bon mots as "Run, Jay and Stupid Bob! Run!" and "Wow—I thought *Chasing Amy* was misguided . . ." (Shit—it's not far from what we're doing with the reels we're watching, adding *Mystery Science Theater*–like comments to the proceedings, catcalling and whatnot. What can I say? We're bitchy little bitches, and it makes the reels a little more tolerable to sit through.) So Sheaks sets about trying to find out if Heather even knows we exist (which I think she does; she auditioned for *Mallrats* many years back;

another reason she may not like us), and if she does, Sheaks promises to lock down a date and time for us to meet-and-greet. No reel is necessary in this instance.

Ever Carradine, however, is a sparkling new talent who hasn't had a breakout role yet, so we need to check out her reel. Yes, she'd been a recurring character on the now-canceled *Veronica's Closet,* and she played the sister on the ill-fated *Conrad Bloom,* but if you're a guy who doesn't watch much TV beyond *The X-Files,The Simpsons,* and sundry other shows that start with "The," you have no idea who she is.

Ever Carradine is the discovery of the day. She's really, really funny on her reel (really, REEL-y funny, one might say; all right, maybe not). She's so good, in fact, that I start wondering how in hell I missed the *Conrad Bloom* bandwagon, and begin questioning my taste in television. We ask Sheaks to set up a meet-and-greet with her promptly.

The viewing party was all we had on the schedule that day, so I opt to take the fam to Disneyland, which some may find ironic, considering the anti-Disney sentiments I've expressed over the last few years. But my

axe was never being ground (grinded?) at Mickey himself. Shit, what Communist robot *doesn't* have a soft
spot for a high-voiced bearer of goodwill with huge
fucking ears and a constant smile (my wife fits the
description too, and I *married* her)? We elect to head
down to Anaheim at one.

But then Affleck calls. He's in his car, between
meetings, and wants to stop by and pick up the new
draft of the script. I tell him to come over, and the wife
nearly shits herself, as she's still in a towel from the
shower, without her makeup on or her hair done. I
remind her that she's married, and that there's little
need to present the best possible aesthetic version of
herself to others anymore (I mean, look at me; the
minute I slapped on that ring, I let myself go by about
fifty pounds, and I was no catch to begin with). She
ignores me, muttering something about keeping her
options open, and proceeds to get gussied up for our
movie star friend.

Here's the truth about Ben Affleck: he may very well
be one of the greatest living human beings of all time.
The man's one of the funniest wits on the planet, one of

the most charming human beings who ever lived, one of the brightest brainiacs never to hold a PhD, one of the most generous fucks around, and an incredible big galoot—all at the same time. It's no secret that I've got a heterosexual crush on him. If I were gay, I'd let him plow my fields of anal gold in a heartbeat. If I were a woman, I'd let him berate me, cheat on me mercilessly, and offer me to his friends as a fuck-toy—so long as he'd stay with me. And if I were a gay woman, I'd think about turning straight for him, or at the very least, let him watch me and other girls munch rug.

As I'm just straight ol' me, I'm simply a fan of the man—personally and professionally. He's one of those cats I could talk to for hours, and usually do, when the opportunity arises. The wife knows this, and is now planning on not getting to Disneyland until six at night.

Affleck arrives and assaults me and Scooter with his infamous bear hugs. Following that, he raids my minibar and starts jawing about *VA5,* as well as his sundry other better-paying gigs: a flick with Sam Jackson he's starting soon, and another flick about a guy from a Tom Clancy book that Indiana Jones once portrayed. Yes—this man who slept on my couch and bitched about how few available chicks there were while we were making *Chasing Amy* can now buy and sell me thousands of times over, thanks to the big, fat movie checks he's earning being one of the most in-demand actors in the biz.

That being said, he's getting paid peanuts to do our picture, another of his shining attributes. From time to time, he'll throw a brother a bone and do a week or two on his little-dick and fart pictures. Thank God the man has loyal tendencies and a heart of gold.

Except when talking about my child.

When my parents-in-law arrive at the room with Harley (my kid), A-fuck proceeds to greet her with a hearty "Hello, little one. I'm your father." Yes, indeed. A helluva guy.

After I throw a script at him and kick him out of my room for besmirching my child's paternity, I and the fam head down to Disney, where we frolic for a little under two hours before the park closes. And call me paranoid, but when I buy myself one of those cool-ass *Sorcerer's Apprentice* hats (complete with Mickey ears), the kid's looking at me like, "I know that man was lying about being my father, Dad, but fuck if I wish it weren't true."

Kevin Smith wrote all that stuff up there. He's making a moo-vie right now, and writing down stuff about a guy who shoots arrows at bad guys for the funny books.

Our Cover Is Blown

MIND YOU, for the purposes of this column, we're still in L.A., but in real life, we're in preproduction already. In fact, last week Dimension put the flick on the schedule officially, as Bob Weinstein (our fearless leader) staked out a date in the summer he felt would give us our best chance at B.O. success (that's "Box Office"; as for Body Odor—well, being really, really heavy, I sweat profusely round-the-clock, so I've got *that* B.O. covered, successfully). The date Bob chose? August 10, one week after the latest Schwarzenegger flick opening (the title of which escapes me, but the plot of which probably has something to do with Arnold shooting *someone* with a very impressive gun), and one week before *Jason X* (presumably another in the long-thought-dead-but-really-just-dormant *Friday the 13th* saga). Bob calls to tell me this the morning of November 9, and the first thing I ask is: "What are you calling it on the schedule?"

Bob says, "What do you mean?"

I say, "Well, we've been calling it *VA5,* so as not to give away the title."

Bob replies, "What the fuck's a *VA5*? And why wouldn't you want to give away the title? The title's one of your strengths, man. Of *course* you want people knowing the title! It's going on the schedule as *Silent Bob and Jay Strike Back.*"

"*Jay and Silent Bob Strike Back,*" I correct.

"Whatever," Bob says. "It's going up today."

Based on that, Miramax/Dimension publicity prepares a press release for the trades, and suddenly, that veil of secrecy we've been shrouding the production in for no real reason other than Lucas does it all the time (and look how well *his* movies do) is yanked off quicker than a horny cheerleader's bloomers at one of those no-boys-allowed-all-girl-on-girl-high-school-experimentation fuck-fests you fantasized about during

those halcyon, thrice-daily days of ardent adolescent
masturbation (which stop when you get married.
Really. Honest.).

But that's all here, in the present. What about where
we left off, back in the past? I believe we were still in
L.A. on our fishing expedition, and it was...

THURSDAY

Thursday, we meet with more actresses, and talk with
Christine Sheaks (our casting mistress) about the
impending Kate Hudson meeting, which is presently
set up for Wednesday morning in New York. Everyone's
happy about this, as she's currently dazzling the press
in *Almost Famous* and taking up more magazine cover
space than a UPC code.

Bob (our fearless leader, and guy with the wallet),
however, is still pushing for the Heather Graham meeting, but Heather's either in London, leaving for
London, or on her way to Morocco (ah, the informa-
tional accuracy of a Hollywood agent). Meanwhile, I'm
still wanting to meet Amy Smart, but the week's almost

over, and she's a no-show. We're repped by the same
agency (the good folks at Endeavor) and they're busting their backs trying to set up this meeting, but Amy's
shooting a picture in Vegas, and may not be able to
make it to L.A. before we leave on Monday. All parties
are biting their nails, when Sheaks tells us that we're
meeting with Matthew McConaughey in the morning.

"Matthew McConaughey?" I ask, dubious as hell.
"You mean *A Time to Kill* Matthew McConaughey?"

"Yeah," Sheaks offers. I notice she says this when
I'm right.

"But he's a big movie star—or at least, *was*—and
this picture's a little beneath him. He just had a hit,
with *U-571.* He certainly doesn't *need* us."

"You're forgetting he's done comedy too," Sheaks
points out. "*Dazed and Confused.*"

"Yeah, and *Larger Than Life,*" Scott points out,
countering Sheaks.

"He's got a point, Sheaks." I nod at Mosier vehe-
mently. "Besides, I don't think the guy knows who we
are, let alone has seen any of our pictures."

"I think it's worth meeting him. Maybe he's a big

fan," says Sheaks. "And then after that, you meet with Charlie Sheen."

"CHARLIE SHEEN?!?" Mosier and I both perk the fuck up.

Mosier grins at me. "MA-SHEEN?!?"

"Mal-catraz..." I grin back.

We're both big *Being John Malkovich* fans.

At that point, we agree to anything Sheaks has to say, because fuck it; she's getting us in a room with Sheen. Anybody who can do that can't be wrong about anything. Ever.

FRIDAY

In the early A.M., I head downstairs to the hotel bar (which is where all the meet-and-greets are taking place), and there sits Matthew McConaughey, arms crossed, decked out in black leather pants, looking chiseled. Mosier's there with him already, and I join the pair, exchange greetings, and talk about Wooderson from *Dazed and Confused* for half an hour. Eventually, he steers the conversation around to the movie we're working on, and asks what it's about.

"It's the movie that closes out the other four we've done," I start. "It's really time, you know; before they overstay their welcome. So we're going to do it with a real balls-to-the-wall comedy, kind of like *Rats,* which tanked. But we're trying to do a little history-correcting here, and make a flat-out comedy that succeeds this time. Plus, the last two were funny but also weighty, and it just feels like it's time to do one that's nothing but funny, with no message or anything, especially after what happened to us on the last one, with all the hate mail and death threats."

It's at this point that I realize Matthew's eyes have glazed over. I can read it in his face: "What the fuck is Tubby here talking about? Close out *what* other four? *Rats*? 'Last two?' Hunhh?"

As suspected, not only is McConaughey *not* a fan, he doesn't know who the fuck we are or what the fuck we're talking about. His agent must've just told him this was a meeting worth having, because (after all) Scott and I have worked with Ben and Matt, so we must be

doing *something* right. In fact, Ben and Matt are coming back on this new, untitled flick too, so maybe it's
worth meeting on.

But as *we* all know, that's just not the case. This is a
slapsticky cluster-fuck of a movie in which Jason
Mewes is the lead. And since Matthew McConaughey
wouldn't know a Jason Mewes if he was pissing on him,
let alone consider playing fourth or fifth billing to him,
this meeting is a complete waste of all of our collective
time. He suddenly knows it, and we suddenly *know* he
knows it. All that's left is for all of us to get out of this
blunder with our dignity intact—which we eventually
do when Matthew excuses himself to go to a far more
important meeting.

Nice guy, really. We just don't show up on his radar at
all. Which is okay, as he doesn't really show up on ours.
We smile, shake hands, and go our very separate ways.

Following that, Mosier and I load into a car and
head over to the CBS/Radford Studios, to meet with a
legend. Bud Fox from *Wall Street*—the man who
brought down Gordon Gekko. A guy who gave the single greatest interview ever given in the rag that is

Movieline magazine, in which he talked about hookers and actors he didn't like. The actor who can steal any flick he's in simply by doing a cameo (see *Ferris Bueller's Day Off* and the aforementioned *Being John Malkovich*).

We go to meet Chuck Sheen.

What Kevin Smith does or has done isn't really important. What is important is that his wife has a really, really sweet ass.

Friday Afternoon
with the Ma-Sheen

MOSIER AND I GO, with script in hand (which is a first, because we haven't given *any* potentially prospective actors the script yet), to the CBS/Radford Studio Lot, where Charlie Sheen is shooting *Spin City*. We're met in the parking lot by his assistant, who leads us to Ma-Sheen's dressing room, where the man who was quoted in a 1994 interview in *Movieline* as warning against sleeping with any costar whose "... pussy smells like her butthole ..." is watching baseball.

Ma-Sheen smiles at us, and we just about melt.

We exchange pleasantries and sit down, mere feet from a guy who once defined the Hollywood fast lane;

the only person in the world Ben Affleck would rather
be than himself (ask him; he'll tell you). But a few
moments into our convo, it's clear that we're no longer
gazing upon *that* Charlie Sheen. *That* Charlie Sheen is
gone. Reformed, some would say. This is the *new* Charlie
Sheen. The *Spin City* Charlie Sheen. The on-his-best-
behavior Charlie Sheen. And while that's probably
good for the life expectancy of Chuck himself, celebrity
journalism has lost one of its bright, shining stars in
the process.

But no man can be a ticking bomb forever. Sooner
or later, we all grow up. And you know what this grown-
up Chuck Sheen says to me?

"You smoke?"

Indeed, I do. Too much. In fact, I'm smoking when
he says this (which is probably *why* he said it).

"I didn't think you were a smoker, because of that
whole antismoking tirade in *Clerks.*"

The man, apparently, knows of my work. Either that
or he'd just watched the first flick, in an effort to familiarize himself with the guys intruding upon his between-
takes down-time (there is a VCR and DVD player there

in the room to support this theory). Regardless, I'm a tickled Japanese schoolgirl in that moment.

Scooter and I fill Chuck Sheen in on what *Jay and Silent Bob Strike Back* is (or *isn't*, depending on who you're talking to), and hand him a script. He says he'll read it this weekend, and then excuses himself to go back to a *Spin City* rehearsal. We shake the hand of the Mighty Ma-Sheen, and head to our car, musing about the odds of him agreeing to do the flick. The role is that of a buffoon, so it's not a guarantee he'll warm to the material at all. But we chuckle about meeting Chuckles all the same, and erect elaborate "What-If?" scenarios in which Sheen does our movie and winds up falling off whatever wagon he's on because of the Jason Mewes influence. This carries us for a good two hours, as Mosier and I are easily amused.

Back at the hotel, our casting mistress, Christine Sheaks, fills us in on Heather Graham: she's in another country, so we're not going to meet her out here. Bob Weinstein wants to send her the script and an offer, but I want to hold out until I've met Amy Smart and Kate Hudson. It looks like Amy's coming to L.A. from Vegas on Sunday, but the Kate meeting has suddenly taken an unexpected turn.

It seems she's suddenly switched representation, leaving her old agency for CAA. The good news is she's now repped by the same agent who reps Ben and Matt. The bad news is we've received word from that agent that Kate will no longer meet with us in NYC. We're to simply make her an offer.

Making an offer means exactly what it sounds like: you tell the actor the part is theirs, if they so desire, and you quote a salary figure. No meet-and-greet or audition is necessary. You're just *that* sure the actor is ideal for the role; so sure that, during the time the offer is extended, no one else is considered for the part.

Now this is strange. We were *scheduled* to meet Kate in New York the following week, but we're suddenly being told that the meeting will not happen. Mosier starts looking into it, as I ready myself for a meet-and-greet with Selma Blair.

I'm a Selma Blair fan. She was the only person worth watching in *Cruel Intentions,* as far as I'm concerned. I've read a few articles about her, and I've seen her interviewed on the KTLA Morning News on a prior trip to L.A., when she was tub-thumping for the WB show *Zoe*... (which was formerly *Zoe Bean,* and then *Zoe, Duncan, Jack and Jane)*. She seems interesting, so I'm way into this meet-and-greet. As it's Friday night around six, I imagine it'll last a mere half hour, because I'm almost certain Selma must have something better to do with her Friday night.

I'm wrong. Selma has nothing to do, so she sits around with me and Mosier for two hours and change. When my wife comes downstairs looking for me (as I've been gone far longer than I said I would be, and she suspects I may have run off with Selma), she joins us, and we sit around for another couple of hours. Why?

Because Selma's a true hoot. All I do is mock her (affectionately, mind you), and all she does is take it. We hit it off so incredibly well that I consider adopting her. She's funny, self-effacing, quick, and honest (i.e., gossipy, although, you've gotta drag it out of her). I want to make a movie with Selma Blair. I want to make a couple movies with her. She's good people.

During our multiple-hour gab-session, she talks

about just finishing up on Todd Solondz's new movie, her proclivity to break up with boyfriends simply by moving to another state, and the actors and actresses she's worked with. When I bring up the *Cruel Intentions* power triumvirate of Sarah Michelle Gellar, Ryan Phillippe, and (Greasy) Reese Witherspoon, Selma's tight-lipped. After much cajoling, however, she finally lets a few stories slip that make this tubby bitch's catty grin spread all the way to the back of his head. They're dishy tales of young Hollywood—so dishy I wish I could relate them here. However, they're not my stories to tell, so I can't go into them. Suffice it to say that Selma, not me, should be given a column.

However, the subject of (Greasy) Reese Witherspoon elicits great interest from me, particulary when Selma informs us that she's been to where (Greasy) Reese Witherspoon and Ryan Phillippe live. I suddenly seize upon an idea so delicious, so asinine and juvenile, that it almost makes the idea of making *Jay and Silent Bob Strike Back* seem Kissinger-statesmanlike in comparison.

With the above closing paragraph, Kevin Smith has just now robbed Stephen King of the title "Master of Suspense." As for what else he's done, who the fuck cares?

The Unholy Tale
of Greasy Reese Witherspoon

IT'S FRIDAY NIGHT AT ELEVEN O'CLOCK, and I, my producer Scott Mosier, and my wife, Jen, are sitting around the patio bar of the Four Seasons Hotel in Los Angeles with *Cruel Intentions* actress Selma Blair. What started as a routine meet-and-greet has now become a five-hour gab session, during which Selma has just let slip that she knows where Greasy Reese Witherspoon lives.

"You must tell me where," I say gravely.

"Why?" Selma asks, a little uncomfortable due to the sudden change in my demeanor, brought on by the mere mention of Greasy Reese Witherspoon.

53

"Because I want to egg her house."

Yes. I *so* want to egg Greasy's house. Granted, I know she's married to Ryan Phillippe, and they have a baby daughter now. But none of that matters to me. We're not talking about a drive-by shooting. We're talking about a drive-by *egging*. I mean, fuck it; it's Friday night, we're in L.A., and we've got nothing else to do. What could be better than whipping eggs at the home of a couple of B-listers?

Now I've got nothing against Ryan Phillippe, mind you. And their baby's in the clear with me too (so far). But Greasy Reese herself? Man, I don't like her. And I'm not talking about her work here (because, like any sane human being with a modicum of taste, I'm a big fan of *Election*; even—as much as I hate to admit it—Greasy's performance in said picture); I'm talking about the *person* Greasy Reese Witherspoon is. I'm talking a *personal* gripe here—more personal than the shark's beef with the Brodys in *Jaws: The Revenge* (or did that infamous tagline refer to the *Brodys'* beef with the *shark*? I could never tell). The reasons for this beef are sundry, and don't warrant getting into here.

Ah, fuck it. Yes, they do.

Waaaaay back when we were casting on *Mallrats,*
Mosier and I are really anxious to meet Greasy Reese
Witherspoon (who I then referred to without the
"Greasy" moniker), because we're both huge fans of the
coming-of-age drama *Man in the Moon.* Back then, our
casting agent, Don Phillips, would meet with the actors
and actresses before we'd audition them, precluding
the meet-and-greets I presently am engaged in all
week. For the Greasy meet-and-greet with Don, Mosier
and I arrange a drop-in, as we're eager to see what she's
like, this young actress who so dazzled us as Sam
Waterston's daughter. So Don is meeting with her in his
office at Universal, and Scooter and I pop in like we
don't know she's there, and start jawing with her. What
a disappointment.

First, she comes off faux-erudite as all hell, and condescending to boot (personality traits that make for the
kiss of death in my book). Secondly, she compares her
Stephen Dorff–starring flick *S.F.W.* to *Clerks,* calling them
"…the same movie, essentially." If you're me, and you've
seen *S.F.W.,* this is tantamount to saying *Clerks* licks balls.

By meeting's end, we tell Don there's no reason to bring her back for an audition, as we're now non–Reese fans.

Now whether this registers at all with Ms. Witherspoon, I have no idea. But on two future occasions, I have run-ins with Reese which are not at all pleasant, and may reflect what one can define as a grudge being held against me for not letting her audition for *Mallrats* (a slight that she should've sent me roses for, all things considered).

The first such run-in takes place at one of *Details* magazine's "Young Hollywood" parties. I'm dragged to the shindig, kicking and screaming (I hate parties, and I hate 'em even more when they're wall-to-wall with creepy young actors in L.A.), by my then-girlfriend, Joey Lauren Adams. We see Reese there, holding court, and Joey wants to extend her a congratulations on her performance in *Overnight Delivery*.

To understand the mammoth gesture this is, you have to know Joey's history with this flick. Many months prior, she and Reese were up for the lead in the picture, on the script for which I did an uncredited rewrite. It was being directed by the same guy who'd also crafted that contender for the cinematic throne of *Citizen Kane, Bio-Dome.*

While *Overnight Delivery* would be unceremoniously dumped straight-to-video by New Line a year later, it was something of a hot project then, and Joey was up for the female lead (indeed, at one point, Joey was going to *not* do *Chasing Amy*—the film that earned her a Golden Globe nomination—and instead do *Overnight Delivery*; and people say there is no God...). Ultimately, Reese was cast instead, as New Line was grooming her for stardom. After the initial understandable bout of disappointment, Joey found peace with this decision, especially once she'd gotten *Amy* under her belt.

So it's a year later. We've shot *Amy* but it hasn't come out yet. Joey and I have seen an early cut of *Overnight Delivery,* and she wants to say something nice about Reese's performance to Reese—a real standup gesture that you'd never catch *me* making, were I in her shoes. We jockey up to Reese (me, quite unwillingly), and Joey tells her that she's seen the flick, and she thinks Reese was really good, adding she's glad

Reese got the part when all was said and done. And how does Reese react?

She sneers at Joey. Then turns away.

Children, I wouldn't say it unless I'd witnessed it with my own two eyes. Greasy Reese Witherspoon sneered at the compliment like the third-grade girl with the most valentines sneers at the third-grade girl with the *second* most valentines after all the valentines have been given out, just prior to the distribution of the holiday cupcakes. It was an ugly, ugly moment. There was no offer of even an insincere, Hollywood-type "Thanks." Merely a sneer.

But *that* doesn't earn her the nickname "Greasy." Reese becomes Greasy when I'm later informed that, on the set of *Overnight,* she quite audibly mocked me.

Me! Radio Raheem!

The mockery was thus: Reese and Paul Rudd (the male lead) are doing the closing shot of the flick, where they walk away from camera. They're supposed to be talking playfully, but since it's understood this is the closing shot (and, presumably, end-credits music will be playing), no dialogue is written. So the director tells the actors to just make stuff up, as it's not going to be heard anyway. What follows is the exchange, as told to me and my elephantine memory (and ass), by someone who was there.

REESE: Who wrote this shit?

PAUL: I think Kevin Smith.

REESE: Ugh! Didn't he write *Mallrats*?

PAUL: Yeah, but he also wrote *Clerks*.

REESE: Who cares? No wonder this dialogue sucked.

Needless to say, when I'm told this, I am livid. Enraged. Mildly amused, yes (hell, it was a good dig), but more enraged.

And from that moment forward, I've never referred to her as anything but Greasy (pronounced "GREE-ZEE") Reese (pronounced "REE-ZEE") Witherspoon (pronounced accordingly).

So when Selma lets slip that she knows where Greasy lives, I'm agog. I'm begging her . . . BEGGING her to give me the address so I can drive by and egg the motherfucker (I'm talking about the house now, not Greasy herself; or am I . . . ?). Selma insists I'll get caught and give her up as the address-provider in the process, but I counter that not only would I *not* give her up, but I'll endure hours of police questioning following my apprehension and still remain zip-lipped.

"So you're already sure you're going to get caught?" she asks.

I offer that getting caught is a *must,* because how delicious is it going to be to have Ryan Phillippe chasing me down the block in his skivvies, all piss and vinegar, after the yolks have hit the fan? And how infinitely *more* delicious will the moment be when *Way of the Gun* catches my ass (which, assuredly, he would, as he's extremely physically fit, and I can barely find the energy to make it to the bowl; unless it's a bowl of Lucky Charms)? I fantasize about him tackling me on a lawn a few yards from his own home (no homoerotic subtext, mind you; the boy's no Affleck), turning me over to see my face, and discovering that the guy who made *Dogma* is the egg-man.

I harp on this for half an hour, but Blair will have no

part of it. Sadly, she eventually heads home, without me having procured so much as a general direction in which Greasy lives.

It is the biggest disappointment thus far on the road to Jay and Silent Bob striking back.

When he's not writing comics and movies, Kevin Smith collects a wealth of matches with which to burn many bridges.

Saturday

THE DAY BECOMES AN EPOCHAL ONE in the
Smith household, for it's the day that I'm to meet
with David Duchovny.

I'm a fan of the man, going back to *The Rapture,* in
which he gives the most haunting delivery of a single
line ever in film. Ever. David plays a swinger who eventually settles down with a Born-Again Christian (portrayed by Mimi Rogers), and the scene I'm talking
about is the one in which a disgruntled employee
David's character recently laid off returns to the work-
place with a shotgun. The guy's icing people left and
right, and he comes to David's office, wielding his
George W. menacingly. David says simply "I have a
daughter." Following that, he's blown away. I can't do

the delivery justice here in print. Check the flick out for yourself and see what I'm talking about.

Of course, I'm an *X-Files* fan as well (indeed, I have two yellow Labrador retrievers named Scully and Mulder). But there is no greater casual *X-Files* fan on this planet ("casual" meaning a fan who won't whip him or herself for missing an episode) than my loving wife, Jen. But more than an *X-Files* fan, she's a Fox Mulder fan. And more than that, she's a Duchovny fan. And when I say fan, I mean she had a little picture of David Duchovny in his tighty-whiteys (that she'd cut out of a magazine many moons prior to meeting me) in her wallet. We were well into the fifth or sixth month of wedded bliss before I eventually asked her to remove it, as ... you know, we were married and all.

So the wife is going ape-shit about this meeting, which *she's* going to as well, running around the hotel room practicing her giggle and hair-flip. It's the only thing I've ever accomplished that she's impressed by, and she's all aflutter. What should she wear? Does she tell him about the dogs' names? Should I (meaning me) stay home?

It's quite emasculating, to say the least.

The meeting came suddenly. His agent called our casting mistress—having heard I was in town, making the rounds—and said that David wanted to meet. Not necessarily to be *in* the movie, as he was doing an Ivan Reitman flick during the time we were to be shooting *Jay and Silent Bob Strike Back.* He just wanted to meet for the hell of it. They also sent over the episode of the *Files* he'd directed last season called "Hollywood A.D.," so that I could familiarize myself with his directorial efforts. It was unnecessary, as I'd not only already seen *that* episode when it aired (in fact, I'd watched it with *great* interest, due to the fact that an article in *Entertainment Weekly* made it sound like there were some minor plot similarities to what I was doing in *Jay and Silent Bob Strike Back)*, but also his directorial *debut* on the show the year before (the great baseball episode with Jesse Martin, he of *Law & Order* fame). I'm up—way up—on the Duchovny oeuvre.

The Ivy in Santa Monica was to be the meeting place, and on the ride there, Mosier filled me in on what had gone down with the ill-fated Kate Hudson New York meet-and-greet.

If you'll remember, Kate's new agent had suddenly informed us that a meeting we were supposed to have with the *Almost Famous* starlet was now *not* going to happen, and we were to, instead, simply offer her the part. I wanted to find out why the sudden shift, when her previous agent had scheduled a meet-and-greet with us a mere few days before. Was it that her new agent felt the white-hot Kate had bigger fish to fry, due to the number of offers he'd been fielding since Cameron Crowe's flick hit the screens? Or was it something more sinister that accounted for the change of heart?

You see, the agent had read the script already. He's one of the few in town who had, solely because he's Ben and Matt's agent, and Ben and Matt are in it. Since he's now also Kate's agent, this *could* mean that he'd judged the project as being beneath her (which, let's be honest, it is; but then, the flick's beneath even Mewes), and he was trying to remove us from Kate's periphery entirely. This irritated me to no end, because even if it's something *he* doesn't want Kate to do, *Kate* should be allowed to decide that for herself.

The question was moot, however, as Kate already

had decided for herself, without needing to look at the script. Mosier had talked to the agent and was informed that Kate's just not really a fan. She doesn't hate the movies, but she doesn't like them either. *She* put the kibosh on the meeting.

Fair enough. Shit, she's not alone. There are many cats out there who don't like our flicks. And truth be told, she wasn't the *best* part of *Almost Famous* anyway. Jason Lee was (but then, I'm biased), and I've already got him in the picture.

That Kate's out of the running means that Heather Graham's casting has lost another obstacle. But I still want to meet Amy Smart before any offers are made. And beyond those two choices, Shannon Elizabeth remains a front-runner (her meeting was just that good, and we continue to be impressed by her, even five days later).

But none of that matters right now, because we're almost at the Ivy. Jen's decided she's not going to sit through the whole lunch. She'll shop for an hour and then "drop in" afterwards. Mind you, she's still trying to perfectly fashion her meeting with Duchovny (because that's what it's become: *her* meeting).

So Jen goes off to shop, and Scooter and I sit down at the Ivy and down some gumbo while we wait for the guy who plays the man who believes the Truth Is Out There. And after ten minutes, the Truth isn't Out There; it's standing in front of us, smiling, saying, "Hi, I'm David."

Kevin Smith drops names like Jason Mewes drops his drawers to total strangers: often and much.

The Tenth
Anniversary Column

THIS IS MY TENTH COLUMN, and I'm celebrating my ability to do over a thousand words each week and still not relate anything even somewhat remotely revealing (or even somewhat remotely *interesting)* about *Jay and Silent Bob Strike Back.* Ah, the ability to say so much without saying much at all. When I'm done with this film crap, I'm heading straight for the political arena where this talent will, no doubt, serve me well (you heard it here first: "Silent Bob" in 2008!).

So it's still Saturday, and David Duchovny has just joined Mosier and me at the Ivy in Santa Monica. It's a lunch during which Mosier says almost nothing, because Dave and I talk about religion and children for almost two hours. We both have new kids, and we both share a passion for the subject of faith. Mosier can lay claim to neither, so he mostly sits there, stirring his iced tea, wondering how two non-Mormons can discuss the Mormon belief system for as long as we do without laughing (at least, that's what I hope he's wondering).

Duchov and I dissect Christianity, Judaism, Satanism, and the rest of the isms. We've both written scripts about religion (me, *Dogma*; him, the *X-Files* episode "Hollywood A.D."), so we do an hour on that subject alone. Then we start in on our kids. Needless to say, Mosier's in Hell.

We gloss over *Jay and Silent Bob Strike Back* because Duchov wouldn't be available for any lead roles in our flick even if he was foolhardy enough to hitch his wagon to our imploding star. He's knee-deep in a flick called *Evolution,* and following that, he still has his remaining *X-Files* episodes to shoot before the potential actors' strike. But his affinity for *Dogma* and his curiosity about Jason Mewes ("Where'd you find that guy? Is he really like that?") has him asking to read the script all the same. I promise to get him a copy.

It's at this point that my wife, Jen, shows up, after having been shopping in Santa Monica for an hour ("shopping" meaning "killing time until she could bum-rush Duchovny"). She joins us and the subject of our dogs comes up. We now have to confess that our two yellow Labs are named Scully and Mulder.

"Oh, that bums me out," David deadpans.

David deadpans a lot. He's a really funny and well-versed guy who I instantly love. There's no bullshit about him—no pretentious air that makes most actors and actresses insufferable. And when the subject of *The X-Files* finally can no longer be avoided, he indulges my fanboy-ism-ness and suffers through my Chris Farley–like probings along the lines of "Remember that time when Mulder was trying to find the truth, 'cause it was out there? That was awesome!" But I don't beat the topic into the ground, because I know personally that cult roles have a way of haunting a motherfucker (ask me how many times people point at me in the mall and say "Fly, fat-ass, fly!" Mind you,

I'm only assuming here that they're reciting the line from *Mallrats)*. Indeed, as we're waiting for our cars outside the restaurant, a guy walks by, points, and says "Whoa! *X-Files!*" Without missing a beat, Duchovny offers, "This is my life."

Then, once Duchov's car is pulled around by the parking attendant and he's about to go, the strangest thing happens: the man writes down his phone number and tells me to give him a call when I'm back in town. "Maybe we can get together with our kids, or just shoot the shit." He shrugs.

Now this is noteworthy because I've never, NEVER had an actor just give me phone number—particularly one who doesn't want something from me. Granted, when Affleck was leaving the set of *Mallrats,* he handed me his digits and insisted that I call him when I got to L.A., as he was, in his words, a "good guy." But this was after we'd shot a movie together, and Ben Affleck was about three years away from becoming BEN AFFLECK. The Duchovny phone number trade falls under a different category altogether, because while we've not spent the last two months shooting a film together, we apparently like each other enough to stay in touch.

And just like that, I've made a new friend.

But the night is young, and there are still even more new friends to make. I head back to the hotel for another meet-and-greet, this time with Eliza Dushku. Some cats may know the young actress as Ah-nuld's daughter in *True Lies.* Some cats may know her as the street-cred cheerleader in *Bring It On.* But most cats would probably know her as Faith, the evil Slayer on those *Buffy* shows.

I've gotta plead ignorant on all counts. I fell asleep during *True Lies* the one time I saw it in the theater; I missed out on the cheerleader flick because the wife cheered throughout high school and felt she'd seen enough sweater meat to last her a lifetime; and I've never watched a single episode of *Buffy.*

Yes, I know. I can hear the collective gasps of *Buffy* fans the world over as they read I'm *Buffy*-challenged. This is, of course, assuming there are at least one or *two* fans of the show who log on to the Internet daily (and before you start feverishly rocketing those "FUCK YU! BUFFY RULZ AND'S GOTS TONS MORE FAN SYTES

THEN YU DO, SILENT FAT CUNT!" e-mails my way, let
me assure you, I'm being facetious; I'm well aware that
the 'net was practically *built* by *Buffy* devotees—as were
Rome, Mount Rushmore, and the Mir space station).
But I missed the *Buffy* boat early on, and since it seems
like the kind of show you have to watch every week in
order to keep up with the breadth of its mythology, I
was always too intimidated to throw myself into the
water and swim after it. Rest assured, when they start
releasing the shows as full-season DVD sets, I'll be
scooping them up like a poseur and pretending I've
been a fan since the pilot's original airing. But until
then, I'm as decidedly *Buffy*-dumb as they come.

On the other end of the spectrum, however, you
have Jason Mewes—my cinematic better half. He didn't
watch the show from day one, but you better believe he
makes up for it now—voraciously. The motherfucker
loves it like Joanie loved Chachi. He builds his life
around *Buffy* night, and the next day, without fail, he'll
ask me, "D'jou watch *Buffy* last night, Moves?"

He calls me "Moves." Long story.

Invariably, I say no, and he launches into a narrative of the episode with all the passion and emphasis that a Ritalin kid who's not been given his Ritalin displays while detailing for his incredulous classmates a Cirque du Soleil performance his parents took him to the night before. I'm talking an incomprehensible line-by-line breakdown of the show in which no character has a name beyond "That one guy who was in that movie we saw once," and "That *American Pie* flute-chick," and, of course, "Buffy"—complete with physical recreations of the slaying techniques exhibited that episode, using me as the vampire stand-in (needless to say, I've been "staked" three or four times a week for the last two years).

But I ain't Mewes (in oh, so many ways, thank Christ), so initially I'm at a loss when I meet Eliza Dushku. Eliza, however, is not the kind of gal who leaves a brother at a loss for long—which Mosier and I discover mere moments after sitting down with her.

Kevin Smith also recently found out that he has a mysterious sister who may or may not really be "The

Key." His current boyfriend also lets vampires suck

blood from him—probably because Kevin, himself,

used to be a Slayer who's still stuck on Angel.

Saturday Night
with Duck-Shoot

ELIZA DUSHKU is that rare breed of cat that most men spend their whole lives searching for: a Guy's Girl, aka: One of the Boys. She's East Coast as all hell, which is refreshing, as I've been in L.A. for almost a week and can use a healthy dose of reality.

A week in L.A.—that's all this column has been thus far. All eleven of these puppies span only seven days that happened over two months ago. It's fucking appalling that I'm getting paid for this drivel. And at the rate I'm telling the story, I'll probably spend the better part of my semi-adult life relating the tale of *Jay and Silent Bob*.

77

Then again, what else is new? That's all I've been doing for the last seven fucking years anyway.

sigh

So there's Eliza, ordering a beer and sitting in the outdoor bar of the Four Seasons Hotel with me and Mosier, waxing vulgar about *Buffy,* Ben (Affleck), and broads (she just kissed one in a movie she recently finished). Her voice has that kind of sexy, raspy quality guys don't mind taking orders from; unless those guys are married—like me—and answer only to one master's voice, particularly when that voice is bellowing "Get off that goddamned Internet and fuck me, Stupid!" Like right now.

Excuse me...

THREE AND A HALF MINUTES LATER
My husbandly duties complete, I return to my story.

I christen Eliza "Duck-Shoot," and we talk about her native country, Boston. She's friends with Casey

Affleck, so she knows Ben—which enables us to swap Ben Affleck stories (my second-favorite pastime to trading Jason Mewes stories). She tries to fill me in on *Buffy* lore and how she plays into the mythos, and it only further solidifies my previously-stated assessment that *Buffy* is a show I should've been into early on, as it's now too intricately told a tale for a latecomer like me to catch up with.

Duck-Shoot's a funny, earthy chick—wise beyond her nineteen years. The fact that she is nineteen causes a bit of alarm, as I've just bought this minor the beer she's quaffing. I suddenly feel like the old man heading into the liquor store who's asked by the carload of teens to buy them a case of Bud and some rolling papers. I insist that I will purchase for her no further brewskis. Twenty minutes later, she suckers Mosier into buying her another. (What can I say? Mosier's a sucker for the raspy voice.)

Right away I want to cast her, because she's funny, familiar, and very East Coast. This is a girl I would've hung out with in high school, back when I was getting dragged to keggers on Friday and Saturday nights. I can tell Mewes and Eliza are going to get along famously, as they both collect friends with weird nicknames. Mewes numbers amongst his comrades a "Neeny-Balls," a "Stink-Weed," a "Mustard," and a "Tic-Tooth Ruth." Eliza regales us with tales of her own hometown chums, who sport equally bizarre monikers. The fact that she spends two hours bullshitting with me and Mosier in her Bostonian "wicked-super"-speak only intensifies my desire to get her into the flick.

When she can no longer tolerate the company of a pair of thirty-year-olds with nothing to do in Los Angeles on a Saturday night, she bids us adieu, leaving Mosier and me to get down to the nitty-gritty of figuring out whether we should shoot in L.A. or Austin. After comparing the budgets and discovering there's only a twenty-thousand-dollar difference between filming in either city, we opt for L.A., as it'll make it easier for most of the cast, who live there, to get to the set. Maybe it's the Catholic in me talking, but I don't want to make it hard on the cast to get to where we're filming this debacle, as I'm lucky most of them even agreed to sign on to our sinking ship in the first place.

SUNDAY

Our last day of casting ends, suitably, with the long-awaited Amy Smart meet-and-greet. Amy's just flown in from Vegas where she's shooting a flick... and boy are her arms tired (see—I can do more than just dick and fart jokes; I'm also gangbusters at the hackneyed material as well). I've only seen Amy in *Road Trip* and *Varsity Blues* (a true guilty pleasure featuring James Van Der Beek uttering that utterly repeatable trailer line I accosted those around me with for months, "I... DON'T WANT... YOUR LIFE!"), but I dug her performances in both of those flicks, so I've been looking forward to this meeting.

Amy's the only actor or actress to show up with a gift: meditation beads. She's apparently into the yoga-type stuff. She's also apparently into Shakespeare, as she tells us she's just spent a few months in England, studying that hard, Bard style of acting. We talk about that, and how she's just done an indie flick with Bob Gale (he of *Back to the Future* screenwriting fame). I give her the dope on his recent comics work as well, including his really good Batman "No Man's Land" issues and the storyline for his forthcoming *Daredevil* run that Joe Quesada filled me in on months ago. It's a fine meeting, but ultimately futile, as Bob (Weinstein) has already let us know that she (Amy) doesn't strike him (Bob) as the kind of person Jay (the character) would fall in love with. He still really wants Heather Graham for that part, and I'm starting to feel bad for wasting Amy's time (the Catholic in me once again rearing its ugly head).

That's the shitty aspect of this job: you can't cast everyone you want. Sometimes, they want nothing to do with you and your stink. Sometimes, the folks you held high hopes for just don't come across well in the meet-and-greet.

Sometimes, you have to listen to what those who hold the purse strings have to say. And sometimes, it rains (a little *Bull Durham* humor for you sports-flick aficionados out there).

The casting process will never be as easy as it was with *Clerks.* Back then, we cast who we felt was the best actor or actress for the job. But that flick was on my dime. When you're playing with someone else's money, you've entered into a collaborative relationship, and other folks get a say. If we weren't comfortable with that, we'd say, "Fuck it—keep your check," and drop to a budget level at which no one can tell us what to do, like we did on *Chasing Amy,* after the studio asked us to cast Drew Barrymore and David Schwimmer in the roles that were written for Joey Adams and Jason Lee. But this time around, the flick's a less personal beast, and not exactly the kind of picture we can make cheaply. So you give up just a smidgen of total autonomy and listen to what the money people have to say.

I can hear some of you Kev-Haters now: "I told you! Fatty's a sellout!" Keep your two cents in your wallet until you're on this side of the table, bellyachers. This is not an evil, soul-selling, integrity-lacking proposition I've entered into with this flick; it's just the cost of doing business on this scale. And believe me, as far as money folks go, Bob and Harvey Weinstein allow for a lot more creative freedom than any other studio head in his or her right mind would afford us (shit, how else can you explain the fact that we're being given millions to make a movie in which I—nonacting-motherfucker me—am one of the lead characters?). But sometimes, art goes out the window (and with this flick, it never even made it into the room in the first place), and cold, simple economics take the floor. Which means that if actor X sells better in the foreign market than actor Y (and they're both equally talented), you'd better believe actor X is going to be the studio fave.

Like Heather Graham. Bob's got it in his head that Heather means something at the box office. And maybe he's right. We'll never know, though, as when we get back to Jersey, the real casting process begins, and Heather presents us with a particularly thorny quandary.

Kevin Smith is really, really tired of talking about
meet-and-greets that happened over two months
ago. He looks forward to dragging this column into
the present after next week.

The Casting Aftermath

WE BID A NOT-SO-FOND FAREWELL to the city of the Angels, and make a break for our home turf (or, as the wife calls it, our "home turd"). Bob (Weinstein) has made up his mind that Heather Graham *must* star opposite Jay and me in the picture, so we send her a script. She's shooting something in Morocco, so it's something of a hassle. After a week, we hear back from her people, who relay the funniest message.

Heather, it seems, likes the script and thinks it's really funny. She won't commit, however, because there's this one issue nagging her about the flick.

Hold on to your socks....

Heather doesn't understand why her character would fall in love with Jay.

I chuckle about this for a day or two. Granted, she's not completely off the mark—I mean, it *is* Jay we're talking about (the character, not the man himself; fuck it—yeah, even the man himself). But then, why does anyone fall in love with anyone in the movies? Shit— why does anyone fall in love with anyone in real life? After all—who can fathom the complexity of the human heart?

Apparently not Heather Graham. My only response to this unanswerable query is "Why did her character fall in love with Austin fucking Powers?" No one else has a response to that one either, but it doesn't matter. The Agents and Managers have gotten involved, as they'd all like to see Heather do this flick. So they start working on her, telling her I'm a good guy, a rising star of sorts, and all manner of other bullshit to help her get past her actress-type question.

Weeks pass.

And more weeks pass.

See, in this business, you can't offer the part to someone else while an actor is already considering it. It's some weird, Hollywood nonsense that can really gum up the works and kill perfectly good preproduction time during which you could be rehearsing another actor in that role. But Bob's holding out hope that Heather's people will convince her to do the flick, so we wait for Heather to make up her mind. My point is, who wants to work with an actress who has to be *convinced* to take the part? After a month, when we're back in L.A. to start preproduction, I finally call Bob and say, "Look, man— can we move on? Me and Mosier want Shannon Elizabeth for the part anyway." And you know what Bob—who's had his heart set on Heather all this time—says?

"Go to Shannon."

And just like that, the whole Heather Graham saga is over. We call Shannon into the office and offer her the part, she says yes, and suddenly we have a leading lady.

The P.S. to the story is that Heather sent me a classy note a few weeks later, thanking me for the consideration, but citing the fact that she's just done four movies back-to-back, and doesn't want to work with me in her exhausted condition. She wishes us well on the shoot, insists we're making a fantastic flick (a fine bit of acting, that), and closes out by telling me I'm "fucking cool." And, since I am a vain man, I buy it hook, line, and sinker, and cross Heather Graham's name off my "Actresses I Must One Day Savage Immaturely in an Internet Column" list. As far as I'm concerned, Graham's a good egg. Confused, but a good egg, nonetheless.

And what about the other cats we met during that week, you ask? Like the legendary Ma-Sheen?

Ma-Sheen read the script and passed. The man who was in more than one *Major League* said that he didn't connect with his character. Fair enough, I guess. It's rare that an actor or actress turns us down (because, in all fairness, we rarely cast people we haven't worked with before), but I'm a big boy (three of you would fit into one leg of my Fat-Boy-Store jeans) and can take it across the chin, balls and all.

But Ma-Sheen just made the fucking list.

Kidding.

Once Ma-Sheen turned us down, I asked if the casting folks would put out the feelers on Will Ferrell. I'm a huge Will Ferrell fan, and after watching *Saturday Night*

Live recently one weekend, it suddenly dawned on me that he'd be a far better choice for the role Ma-Sheen couldn't connect with. A call was made, and a meeting was set up at the Tribeca Grill in Manhattan. Will and I got along well, and I gave a script to the man who has single-handedly kept my interest in *SNL* going for the last few years (I can watch him impersonate deceased sports announcer Harry Carey for hours, get a good night's sleep, wake up, and watch him do it all over again for another few hours). Two days later, we were told he loved it and was in. Needless to say, I was ecstatic.

We found a place for Ever Carradine, and then made room for Judd Nelson as well. For the latter, I'm currently rewatching *The Breakfast Club* so I can crib some obscure Bender lines for my script. You can call it homage, but I call it flat-out theft of grade "A" material for capitalization on a successful film (certainly isn't the first time I've done it; there are dopey fucks out there who think I actually came up with the line "Adventure? Excitement? A Jedi craves not these things.").

Then there were cats we didn't meet, but who wound up being in the flick regardless. We heard that

Seann William Scott (he of "Stifler" fame) was a fan, so we offered him a part. He gladly obliged us, and when I talked to him on the phone, the man told me he had a framed *Mallrats* poster in his house. I was taken aback, as *I* don't even have a framed *Mallrats* poster in *my* house. Say what you will about our redheaded stepchild of a second film, but it has its fans.

Tracey Morgan is my other reason to watch *SNL*, and nine times out of ten I'm crushed by disappointment because they never give the guy enough airtime. So when I was writing the script, I wrote a small but funny bit for him. The meet-and-greet wasn't necessary, as I knew I wanted Tracey in the flick. We offered him the role and, thankfully, he accepted it.

Jason Biggs, too, jumped on—thus making this movie the unofficial sequel to *American Pie* (what with Seann and Shannon already in place). I told him all the pie-fucking scenes were reserved for Mewes in this movie, but he didn't seem to mind. I was delighted to learn that he's a Jersey boy too, meaning that even though we're shooting the lion's share of this opus in L.A., Jersey will, indeed, represent.

The Smith Family is also going to represent, as not only am I going to be in the picture, but so, too, are my kid and my wife. That's right—the woman I fuck and the product of our lust will be making their big-screen debuts in *Jay and Silent Bob Strike Back.* Jen has a pretty big part (which she's earned by taking my very little part nightly), and Harley pops up in a fairly prominent (and fitting) role herself. You can do these kinds of things when you're the boss.

So along with those cats mentioned, we've also got the returning players: George Carlin, Jason Lee, Brian O'Halloran, Jeff Anderson, Ben Affleck, Matt Damon, Chris Rock, Mewes, me, and sundry others. There are a few more casting surprises I don't want to talk about until their deals are done, but there is *one* I'll spill on because it's just too cool not to share.

When I got back to L.A., I called David Duchovny, as instructed. He invited the wife and me and our baby to his house to chill with him and his wife ("Tea" something) and their adorable kid. Since he'd expressed interest in reading the script, I brought a copy with me to lay on him. Two days later, he called and said he laughed out loud reading it, which I took as a compliment, opting not to dig for further details as to whether he was laughing *at* it or *with* it. Duchov cleared up the mystery by saying he'd love to come aboard for a small role he fell in love with in the script.

I was floored. Needless to say, the wife doused her drawers.

So at press time, we're trying to make the schedule work in a way that'll allow the ever-busy David to come out and play. No promises here, because once he's finished with *Evolution* (the movie he's currently shooting), he has to go back to *The X-Files.* And as much as I'm salivating over having the brother in our picture, I'm not going to be the guy who fucks with Mulder showing back up on the *Files.* I like our movie a lot, but shit—I'm an *X*-fan first. Keep your fingers crossed that we can work it out.

Kevin Smith is a very, very lucky sumbitch.

PART TWO

Jen's Painting

SO A FEW NIGHTS AGO, I'm at a Hollywood gathering, standing there with a couple of other people, staring at my naked wife, and we're all commenting on how good she looks, but none of us wind up fucking her.

Let me explain...

About six months back, Jason Lee (he who's essayed the roles of Brodie, Banky, and Azrael in the films I've made) invited me and the wife to a showing of the work his artist friend Bryten Goss had thus far painted. Outside of a comic book art exhibit at the now-defunct Four Color Images in Manhattan, I'd never really been to an art exhibit, so I was mildly curious to check out the scene. Since it's an L.A. art exhibit, my wife is wetting her thong to do the same.

See, the wife had lived in L.A. for seven years when I first met her. She'd interviewed me for that venerable bastion of the Fourth Estate, *USA Today*, and we wound up hitting it off pretty well after the Qs and As were out of the way. We'd eventually gotten to know one another in the biblical sense, and Jen (my wife) decided that she'd come to Jersey to live with me, so that we might continue our newfound mutual interest in fucking the shit out of one another between expressing "I love you"s. Once Jen got to Jersey, however, she began to wonder if I was even that good a lay (and, trust me: I'm not), as the differences between life in Los Angeles, California and life in Red Bank, New Jersey are about as drastic as the differences between life in London and life in Newcastle. She'd signed on for romance, and she'd gotten a shit-load of coal.

So since she spends most of the year trapped in Jersey, wondering how the fuck a fat-ass fashioner of marginally successful films who isn't hung very well at all Jedi-Mind-Tricked her into leaving Paradiso for Purgatorio, whenever we're in L.A. on business or something and we get invited to an even semi-interesting event, I humor the wife and attend. This art show, I believed, would be just one of those nights.

Now I was picturing something Bohemian: a run-down garage with a handful of impressionistic bullshit hanging from the walls, all being nodded at by faux-hipsters who'd pay far more money than the scribblings were worth, simply out of pretension and the need to feel even remotely connected to the arts. After all, this is Los Angeles we're talking about; there is not art of any kind in Los Angeles . . . unless you include the art of making horrible fucking movies, the art of narcissism, the art of pursuing eternal youth via painful surgical procedures, the art of tossing out the perfect bon mot to *Entertainment Tonight,* or the art of self-importance as a way of life.

Upon arrival at the event, though, my impression of what the show would entail proved completely naive, as *InStyle* magazine was our host for the evening, and there were celebs galore and a red carpet entry, complete with over a hundred paparazzi, clicking away at the likes of Nic Cage and Jenna Elfman. I'd seriously overestimated L.A.'s ability to do anything subtle, so my vision of an impromptu, beatnik gallery had to be extended to include sound-bite-catchers jamming tape recorders into my face, asking me who I was "wearing."

Once past the melee, however, I was delighted to learn that I was even more off-base on what the show would be—as what was hanging from the wall weren't merely depictions of boring geometric shapes that screamed "First Year at Art School!" Far from it, lads and lasses.

They were nudes.

And I'm not talking flirtatious little etchings of sun-dappled cherubs either; I'm talking huge, fuck-off, six-foot renderings of honest-to-goodness naked ladies. And these weren't impressionistic nudes with mis-shapen heads and shit. Fuck no—these were figure-studies, so they were photo-realistic. I was standing in the midst of a roomful of famous people, looking at a slew of life-size, bare-assed broads.

This was an L.A. I could get behind.

And that's when the wife dropped the bomb.

"I want to do it," she said, staring up at the paintings.

"What...here?" I asked, wondering if I could pull off public coitus.

"No—I want to get a nude painting and hang it in our room."

"Are you sure it isn't too early in our marriage to start bringing other naked chicks into our bedroom?"

Very witty, Wilde; very witty.

"I don't want one of *these*," she explained. "I want one of *me*."

Then she looked at me very seriously and said...

"I want to get painted in the nude."

Off my confused and worried look, my wife continued. "You have your whole career, a modicum of critical respect, cult fame..."

Oblivious to where she was going with her rationale, I asked, "You think I only get a *modicum* of critical respect?"

"I don't have my own *thing* anymore. I don't have something that's uniquely my *own;* something that's *not* connected to you somehow. I think it's important that I do something like this for *me*."

See, believe it or not, *USA Today* doesn't have a New

Jersey bureau—which means that when the wife moved, she gave up her career in journalism. And because my job dictates the course our life takes, most of what we have/do/talk about has to do with me and my stupid movies. My wife wanted something in her life that didn't have anything to do with me, and in a weird way, I understood that. And since a painting is a lot less heartbreaking than her simply going out and having an affair, I'd have to be an idiot to argue against it.

So I said, "Okay."

We hooked up the details and headed to Bryten's apartment about a month later. Step one in the process was simple: Jen had to peel down to her pubes so Bryten could take reference pictures of her from which he could work. Gone were the days of subjects sitting stone-still for weeks while an artist attempted to capture their essence. In the digital age, a few tawdry snapshots would do.

But the whole drive over, the wife was nervous like you read about.

"What the fuck was I thinking?! I can't do this," she

fretted. "I can't take my clothes off in front of some stranger and let him take my picture!"

"Sure you can," I offered, attempting to steel my wife. However, unbeknownst to her, I was in agreement with her initial assessment. I knew my wife pretty well, and while she's no prude, she's pretty anal about people —even me, after almost three years of marriage— looking at her body too closely. As we elevatored up to Bryten's apartment, I began to wonder how long we'd be there before she chickened out.

Proving once again that I don't know shit, two glasses of wine after our arrival, my wife was standing before a backdrop, utterly nude, offering the camera better come-hither attitude than any half-*dressed* runway model I'd ever seen. I suddenly felt as conservative as a church pipe organist. And, mind you, I made *Clerks*.

Jen was in all her glory (physically and psychologically) at the front of the room, Bryten was between us, snapping pics of my wife like she was one of those porno stars at the Cannes Film Festival who waltzes into the midst of the paparazzi and drops her gear, and I was sitting in the back of the room, staring wide-eyed at the scene, wondering how the fuck I got there from working in a New Jersey convenience store all those years ago. And while it was a little odd "sharing" my wife like that over the course of two hours, I've gotta admit, it was quite the turn-on. I mean, I was given a better look at Jen than I'd ever been afforded before. She'd never paraded around in the flesh like this at home, and the few times I had caught her in the buff and attempted a firm, leering once-over of every inch of her body, she'd quickly covered up and ushered me out of the room.

But that wasn't the case that night. That night, I was able to visually pore over every nook and cranny of Jen's form without her feeling self-conscious. And I took her in like an all-you-can-eat visual buffet. I studied her defining ears, her sincere eyes, her pouty (and sometimes potty) mouth, her perfect neck, her pinky-sized nipples, her flat stomach, her beckoning lips (you know the lips I'm talking about . . .), her sublime, heart-shaped ass, and her long, luscious legs.

This was my life-partner, and as I drank her in, I realized she was more beautiful than I'd ever suspected. This was my soul-mate fully exposed in such a way that I was able to gain a smidgen of insight into her incredibly complex psyche that I hadn't been privy to before. This was my best friend, the person who would forever define me. This was the mother of my child, and the keeper of all my tomorrows.

And this was one hot-lit piece of ass who was giving me a boner like you wouldn't believe.

So months later, we're standing in Bryten's apartment again, staring at the result of that photo session: a six-foot-tall rendering of all the beauty, eroticism, and self-confidence I'd witnessed the night my wife was waltzing around as naked as my ambition. It was a classy, sexy, and very expensive reminder of not only how much I love Jen, but also how content I am to turn a blind eye to all other women and fetishize, solely, my wife.

And Jen fell in love with the painting, but not in the same way Narcissus fell in love with his reflection. Seeing herself frozen in time in oils on canvas excited her, yes; but it also gave her a sense of peace. She had her one thing that wasn't predicated on anything I'd done. This painting was now an heirloom—something that'd be passed on to future generations of our family. And as someone who's used to living in the shadow of Silent Bob, Jen seemed elated to have something that would make *her* immortal. Sure, our great-great-grandkids *might* talk about me and the flicks I'd made, once I'm dead and gone; but they'll *definitely* talk about Jen, and her unabashed portrait.

And while I haven't asked her yet, I got the distinct impression as I looked at my wife looking at a nude painting of herself that she felt relieved. Because even though the present was filled with me and my bullshit, the future belonged to her. Ultimately, I was a flavor of the month, while she was now firmly established as timeless and classic.

So I wasn't exactly honest at the head of this piece. A few nights ago, I *was* standing there with a couple of other people, and we *were* staring at my naked wife, commenting on how good she looked...

But one of us *did* wind up fucking her later that night.

Guess who?

Britney

SO LAST NIGHT, I'm flipping through the multiple-channel vista that is digital cable, and I see something that suddenly makes me feel very old and very prude.

There was a Britney Spears concert on HBO.

Now, until this point, I hadn't paid much attention to that veritable force of nature, Hurricane Britney—much like I don't pay attention when an earthquake ravages some foreign nation that isn't Red Bank, New Jersey. Like that earthquake, Britney Spears was just some shit that happened over *there*—even though *there,* in this case, wasn't abroad, and was instead on the pop cultural landscape that's supposed to be within my purview. However, as I sat there, captivated by what

I saw (or rather, the *lack* of what I saw), Britney Spears finally heaved those enormous cans she's so proud of onto my radar, and I immediately set about analyzing and overanalyzing what it is that draws people to her.

Mind you, I'm only going off of the five to ten minutes I watched before changing the channel (and, as we all know, five to ten minutes is generally the amount of time any passerby can stare at a car wreck before they've gotta get on with their own, vital lives), but from that brief glimpse into the Spears-o-scope, I quickly discovered something kind of horrifying.

Britney doesn't sing.

Yes, I realize that at some point, Britney (or however many Britneys studio technicians can generate) had to have warbled the songs that made it onto whatever album she's currently pimping (or should that be *whoring?*). However, in *concert,* it would appear that Britney isn't singing. She simply lip-synchs—and badly, at that. She jumped the gun on some lyrics, and missed the beat on a few others. It was like watching karaoke, to some degree—particularly when the person doing karaoke loses their place mid-song, and they stand there, staring at the screen, reading the lyrics silently, trying to catch up. But, shit, Britney wasn't even on the level of a karaoke caroler, as even people doing karaoke actually *sing*.

And this didn't take Sherlock Holmes to figure out, either. Fuck, it wouldn't have even taken Watson. Even someone deprived of sight from birth could tell there was no live singing going on during the "live" show, as the songs sounded exactly as they do on the radio, with zero impromptu deviation. But I was nonetheless astounded to see the audacity of this songbird who stands on stage and, apparently, never intones a single note. Now, granted, she was gyrating up a storm, and it's difficult to sing and dance at the same time (hell, with my girth, it's difficult to talk and walk at the same time). But it can be done. There are those who've made a comfortable living performing elaborate dance routines *while* singing at the same time. Honorary Brit Madonna does it, and she's almost fifty, right?

So why the fuck would anyone want to watch someone *pretending* to do her job? Since there are those of you out there who are no doubt posing the question right back to me ("Why would anyone want to watch the films of someone who pretends to be a director, Kevin?"), I'll use myself as an example of how, in some cases, the artist (a term I'm not comfortable applying to either Ms. Spears or myself) transcends the art they make.

In some cases, I can say, without a hint of shame, that there are folks who like to watch my stuff because they like *me.* My mother's an example of that, yes; but beyond my mom, there's a whole portion of the audience who aren't fans of the flicks as much as they are supporters of me, personally. How does that happen? Well, I spend inordinate amounts of time at my company's website, interacting with people who like the flicks, and beyond that, I do panels at three or four big comic book conventions and numerous college Q&A's per year. This gives anyone who's even remotely interested in my bullshit ample opportunity to get to know the real me (or, at least the "me" I present). And if the performer puts enough of himself or herself out there that the audience can identify with, the work—and the quality of the work—sometimes takes a back seat. It can sag a little, so long as they like you.

So, if it works for me, I figured maybe *that's* what draws folks to Britney: the identity factor. They feel close to Britney because they *know* Britney. Perhaps she, too, puts herself out there for her fans, and I just hadn't heard about it. And thankfully, I was given an opportunity to gauge this when Britney took time out from pretending to be a live singer to have a heart-to-heart with the audience.

She sat at a piano and, microphone in hand, told the audience how she's living her dream every day—by which, I can only assume, she meant that she can't believe she makes this much money showing off her belly button a lot and pretending to croon on stage. She followed that with a bit of homespun advice that people should never stop dreaming. Nothing too deep there, but nothing dishonest either. It's a simple message, yes; but sometimes, simple messages bear repeating for the masses—especially if they come from the heart of the speaker.

However, as she was so obviously reading the entire

speech from a teleprompter, that wasn't the case.

It was not a heart-to-heart so much as a pre-programmed, double-checked, and cleared through BritneyCo. collection of quasi-positive propaganda. The girl very visibly read her sentiments in a fashion that only a child could ignore—which then led me to surmise that, perhaps, Britney is just kid's stuff. Maybe she's nothing more than a harmless bubblegum pop-ster, with a predominantly pre-teen audience. With that, all my dissection of Brit-ania suddenly seemed like it was for nought, as, apparently, the Phenomenon du Spears is meant solely for a demographic I'm no longer a part of. Let the young 'uns have her, I fig-ured—as it's the province of children to adhere blindly and loyally to figments of imagination. Like Santa Claus and the Easter Bunny before her, they'd grow out of Britney eventually.

But a few camera pans of the audience later revealed that this wasn't the case either. The audience wasn't made up of little girls and boys, barely out of diapers at all. It was made up of people like me (though much thinner)—folks who are supposed to be older and wiser. And these weren't just womenfolk, either. There were tons of guys my age holding up makeshift signs, declaring their allegiance to the non-singing product on stage. And since these folks aren't really interested in seeing Britney sing live (because she doesn't, apparently), I came to my ultimate conclusion on the subject.

People are into Britney Spears because they want to *fuck* Britney Spears.

Okay, *that* I get. She wears very little clothing, and plays up the barely-legal, come-hither thing with more aplomb than Sue Lyon in Kubrick's *Lolita*. She purrs "Not a Girl, Not Yet a Woman" as if she's daring the listener to be the first on the block to make a grab for her panties. She hurls her are-they-or-aren't-they boobs around like "blodgers, trying to knock the Harry Potter of our libido off his Nimbus 2000 and into her engorged labia. She maintains she's still a virgin in the same winking fashion that Bush said he wanted Bin Laden dead or "...alive." And to top it all off, she's a blonde, southern gal—that legendary farmer's daughter, who beckons us out to the barn for a roll in the hay ... or at least a sloppy blowjob behind the pigpen.

And this is when I started feeling old. Because, I'm sorry—but I don't get turned on by a high-schooler who's just figuring out her feminine wiles (well, *not anymore,* at least). Those days are long-gone. I can't fetishize a teenage girl at my age; all I can do is wonder why more of them didn't turn out to see *Jay and Silent Bob Strike Back.* Anyone over the age of consent who's ogling this nymphet needs to be prohibited from driving by day care centers—because if they're getting stiff for Britney, sooner or later, they're going to want them even younger. These pederasts-in-waiting need to be jailed and re-educated now, before they start menacing our sons and daughters.

As for Britney? Well, she's harmless. She's a marketing ploy. She's a fad with legs, and as soon as some even chestier eleven-year-old with a halfway decent voice figures out how to work some simulated fellatio into her act onstage without getting arrested and sent to juvenile hall, Britney will seem quaint.

I'm sure some of you are saying "I can't believe this potty-mouthed cretin who's made a living out of dick and fart jokes dares to get all prude about Titney Spears?" Rest assured, I'm no prude, okay—anyone who's seen my flicks can attest to that. But when I want to see someone sing, I want to see someone sing. When I want something to masturbate to ... I'll just ask my wife to bust out her vibrator and show me how she really wants to get fucked, while she fingers her ass and tells me in extremely vulgar terms what a lousy lover I am.

What can I say? I'm a conservative guy at heart.

The Letters

I'VE ONLY WRITTEN TWO COLUMNS for *Arena* thus far: one was about the Britney Spears phenomenon and how I don't get it, and the other was about a nude painting of my wife I commissioned. The feedback I've read to the pair of pieces has further reinforced my suspicion that when I ply my trade as a writer, people either love me or just fucking hate my guts.

Cases in point: amidst all the business-related missives, autograph requests, and personal back-and-forths that litter my e-mail in-box on a daily basis, last week I found these two incredibly diverse reactions to the columns. Together, they really sum up the spectrum of responses to anything I do.

I'm withholding the names and e-mail addresses,

but other than that, I present them to you in their entirety. Both authors are males.

This first reaction is in regards to the second column, about the painting of my wife, Jen.

> *I just wanted to drop a line and say how wonderful it is to read a man writing so passionately, lovingly, and understandingly about his wife. It is so rare for me to come across somone who can accurately articulate how I imagine many men must feel about their wives, and I think it is wonderful that Kevin saw fit to share his love and wonder with the rest of us. I love the films, but I am increasingly hoping that he will sit down and start writing books sometime. He has a gift for expressing in succinct terms ideas that have driven poets for all of history—not to minimize those great men and women, but it is an all too rare talent in this day and age. Keep up the fantastic work.*

Nice stuff, that. Made me feel good about myself, and my decision to delve into my personal life in print. I read that, and I feel all warm inside.

Then I read the next one.

This reaction, as you'll learn pretty quickly, is in regards to the first column I wrote for *Arena*—the one about Britney. The BBS the outraged author is referring to is the message board at my website, www.viewaskew. com.

> *I registered with your BBS but I couldn't wait for my 'password'.*
>
> *I just want to tell you what a complete waste your articles in Arena are. I cannot imagine what these pathetic fools are paying you to be their token hipster, but please let them know I would be willing to waste print space with my personal diatribes for HALF of what they pay you.*
>
> *First, let me set you straight on a few things. Piss and moan about Britney Spears all you want, it just proves what a pussy-whipped eunich you are. ANY MAN who would look at Britney and not lust is either a flaming Homersexual, or trying to earn gimme points from his missus.*
>
> *Is that it? Does your wifee find Britney particu-*

larly threatening to her self image so you're buttering her buns in a national magazine? You come off as ridiculous, given your track record, bad-mouthing Britney and her fans and then tossing Mewes as your 'best pitch'? PLEASE! You think watching those absolutely HORRIBLE cut scenes of you and Mewes hanging at 'your pool' in the Clerks video is somehow preferrable, or more HONEST, than Britney lip-syncing her new number?

If you want to see cool guitar licks go see the Who, you idiot!

If you want to see a great musical performance go see Ray Charles, you moron!

When people want to see a barely-legal piece of prime USDA-grade pseudo jailbait, let us have our Britney!

First you cave to the gays, now you're trying to get 'street cred by' attacking Britney Spears? What's next Rosie, are you gonna start bad-mouthing the 2nd Amendment?

Too bad you couldn't get that artist to paint you a pair of balls with your wife's portrait you shrimpy-

dicked loser! I've never given a penny of my money for anything Britney, but she sure graces my monitor wallpaper! You can't even write a movie without references to dick smoking and you call ME a pedophile because Britney's hot?

You are losing it, fat man.

P. S. Oh, and one more thing. It has been YEARS since I saw Chasing Amy, but I happened across it last night channel surfing and it left me in physical PAIN to watch! I came toward the end with the big diatribe Minney Mouse was giving to Holden about the three-way. It just went on, and on, and ON! Getting ass-fucked by Banky would be preferable to sitting through that over-dialogued bit of shmegma!

You really are the luckiest man in the world, aren't you?

Well . . . yes. Yes, I am the luckiest man in the world. And here are five reasons why.

1)   *Arena* lets me blab on in their magazine about any-

thing I want on a monthly basis. God Bless *Arena* magazine.

2) There are still people like the first letter-writer who employ the wonder of the Internet to give a total stranger a pat on the back, as opposed to the legion of bitter armchair quarterbacks with enough free time on their hands and rectums full of dashed hopes that perpetually burn their asses, because the only recognition they'll ever get is for being anonymous, whiney, "Why You And Not Me?" poison-pen fuckers.

3) Apparently, Justin Timberlake of *NSYNC reads my columns. I mean, it's gotta be Justin Timberlake writing that vitriolic (and funny, too, I'll admit; I've taken to including the term "shrimpy-dicked loser" in all of my conversations lately) mess, right? Because Justin Timberlake is at least *dating* Britney Spears. And nobody who isn't *at least* dating Britney Spears could possibly be that defensive about Britney Spears, could they?

4) As long as I'm the one with the column, I'll always

have the last word over the shrimpy-dicked losers
of this world (see?).

And most importantly:

5)   That guy did the lion's share of the work for me this
     month, and I just got paid for printing his letter in
     my column.

Yes—I am, indeed, the luckiest man in the world.

Morbid Obesity 1

THERE'S AN OLD BILL COSBY BIT that details a bout of tonsillitis he endured when he was a kid. It's genius stuff, in which a young Bill is suckered into a tonsillectomy under the half-false pretense that in exchange for an overnight hospital stay, during which he'll surrender his tonsils, the young patient will then be given all the ice cream in the world he can eat. What he learns, of course, is that once his tonsils are lopped out of his throat, his interest in eating ice cream dwindles substantially.

And, like most practical matters in life that I have a passing familiarity with, that was the extent of my knowledge on the subject of tonsillitis. The curse of living in America is, from a young age, you're saddled with this lazy presumptuousness. That is to say that, rather than being well-versed on a subject, most of us on this side of the pond are content to bluff our way through it, based on what little we know about the subject—all while posing as experts in the field. If we hear one or two sentences in regard to, say, cave exploration, we then present ourselves to the world as well-heeled spelunkers.

Where I think this kind of boastful ignorance might be most noticeable is in the bedrooms of most American men, as they consider themselves such great lovers, while, in fact, the opposite is usually true. Based on grade school conversations about sex they overheard from their older brothers (or, worse, based on information their *friends* maintain they overheard from *their* older brothers), most Yank boys grow up without a clue as to how to go about getting their girlfriends off. And since further education on the subject would have been warranted in order to learn the nuances of a woman's body, most teenagers I knew were content to never investigate the tricks of the trade any further—because, y'know, they knew *everything* about fooling around with girls already.

This proved a huge sexual boon for me from puberty to the altar—because all these Neanderthal leg-humpers wound up doing was producing a nation of women looking to get off properly. This has always given me a much-needed sexual edge over the alpha males; and it's been an edge I've always needed, based on my aesthetic appeal. As an overweight teen, I should've been doomed to late-night dick-handling to some titty flick on cable as my only sexual outlet. But while I soiled my share of tube socks over many a late-night dick-handling to titty flicks on cable (I mean, I was a teenage guy; that's what we *did)*, it was in *addition* to *always* being able to not only secure passage into the pants of my distaff peers, but also the ability to woo them away from their boyfriends. And this wasn't because I was attractive in the traditional sense, heavens no. This was largely because a brother can get pretty far on a good sense of humor and a great knowledge of what stimulates the clitoris. While most of my fellow high school brethren were laboring under the misconception that their girlfriends relished nothing more than a rapid-fire, semi-dry finger-banging as foreplay, the fat kid who actually *owned* a book on gynecology when he was thirteen and bothered to educate himself on *how* the vagina worked, was the dark horse backseat lover; the guy who got more pussy than he probably should have, looking like he did.

But resting on one's laurels isn't always the healthiest option either, as I quickly learned in the ear, nose, and throat specialist's office last week.

First off, I was informed that the sore throat which had prompted my visit was, indeed, tonsillitis. My assumption that I'd go under the knife and then receive all the ice cream I could eat in the world was met with the unromantic reality that tonsillectomies are rarely peformed anymore, as antibiotic treatment of the condition will usually remove tonsillitis-related throat irritation within twenty-four hours of diagnosis. So much for my proposed best-seller, *Everything I Know in Life, I Learned from Bill Cosby.*

But the good doctor didn't stop with the prescription-writing there, oh no. Based on his look-see into my gaping maw, he also discerned that I suffer from what I used to call heartburn, but now call Acid Reflux Disorder. It's a condition which develops due to far too much digestive acid being produced in the stomach, which then splatters upwards, burning the esophagus. The doctor prescribed something to be taken at bedtime that would eventually cure this condition, as simply taking Rolaids wasn't enough anymore, and stemming acid reflux was a sure-fire way in which to avoid esophageal cancer.

"How'd I develop this?" I asked, fascinated to learn about the high drama going on in my gut.

But I wasn't at all prepared for his response.

"It's often associated with cases of morbid obesity."

I nodded first, because I wasn't really listening. I was still dwelling on the esophageal cancer. But after a beat, the doctor's words sank in.

"I'm sorry—did you say morbid obesity?" I inquired, brow furrowed.

"Yes—your weight falls into the category of morbid obesity."

"What does that mean?"

"You're a smart guy. You know exactly what it means. As heavy as you are, you're taxing your heart substantially more than most normal people. Throw in the smoking, and you're dangerously unhealthy for someone your age. You've gotta drop weight and lay off the cigarettes or you're going to die very young."

What the fuck? I went in there with a sore throat, and I came out of there with a foot in the grave.

He prescribed me something called Xenical, a pill that prevents 30% of the calories you digest from being stored as fat. Taken in conjunction with a low-calorie diet, one could expect ten pounds of permanent, healthy weight loss a month (though how healthy the weight loss could be with a chemical compound involved that tricks the body into *not* doing something it does naturally is questionable). With a smile, and a "Lose some weight so you can watch your kid grow up, huh?" I was sent on my way.

"How the fuck could this have happened?!" I asked myself as I stumbled out of the doomsayer's office. But I knew the answer, really: this was laze of the highest order, both physically and psychologically. I mean, the only time I ever ran around in the last ten years was when I was dressed up like Silent Bob and it was called for in a scene. Short of that, I haven't exercised in years.

It also didn't help when Jen got pregnant. We're

talking about a tall, slender, vain woman watching herself get "fat" with child. While she never came out and requested it, she needed someone to get fat right along with her. But nine months later, when Jen delivered our daughter, Harley, my wife dropped back down to her normal size (and rather quickly at that), while the "baby" I was carrying—the one comprising all manner of junk food—never came to term, and simply continued to sit in my gut. And rather than do something about it, I just kept feeding it, and feeding it, and feeding it, until one day I looked in the mirror and said, "Wow—that guy looks like me, only sixty pounds heavier." But rather than immediately implement an exercise/weight-loss regimen, you make these excuses and deals for and with yourself.

"You're married to a good-looking woman, and she's not complaining about your weight," I've said to myself on occasion. "It's not like you're trying to fuck anyone else, right? So if it ain't broke, don't try to fix it. Shit—you've got this great, high-profile job in which you prove on a daily basis that quick wits and a clever turn of phrase will always win out over tight abs and buns of steel.

You're throwing the whole aesthetics-conscious curve in this silly business, man. You're a rebel. You're standing up for the little guys against a societal obsession with being thin that's so sick and far gone that it produces bulimics and anorexics. So long as you don't gain any more weight, I don't see what the problem is."

I'm not kidding—I've actually *had* that conversation with myself. How insane am I?

Not nearly as insane as I was waiting in line for my prescription, I'll tell you that.

"Good God, what do I tell my wife? How could this have happened? Why didn't anyone ever say anything? My left arm feels tingly—isn't that usually the first indication of a heart attack? All that, and I've yet to turn in my *Arena* column!" These were the thoughts that plagued me all afternoon....

Until I read the "Cautionary Warnings" on the bottle of Xenical, which promised one of the most disturbing side effects in the history of modern medicine.

Morbid Obesity 2

THERE WAS THIS EPISODE of "The Simpsons" in which Homer learned that if he gained a lot of weight, the power plant would have to make arrangements for him to work from his home, unable to fire him simply for being fat. So Homer starts eating away, eventually blowing up to three hundred and fifteen pounds, at which point he doffs the white shirt and blue pants of old, and dons a less clingy, more comfortable piece of clothing instead: a muumuu.

I, too, have a muumuu. It's this sleeveless, hooded blue sweatshirt that I've been wearing for about two years now. Hours of sweat and wear and tear have made the print on the tag in the collar all but invisible, but if you look closely at the faded text, you can make out a few X's. Many people have asked why I wear the sweatshirt so much and where I got it. For years, I've told them it was my rebellious fashion statement, and that I wasn't quite sure where I got it. Neither of those claims are true.

I wear that sweatshirt because (I believe) it hides my gut.

I bought it at one of those Big and Tall stores.

It may sound stupid, but admitting to those two more-than-likely-apparent-to-everyone facts may just save my life.

Last month, I detailed my adventure at the ear, nose, and throat specialist, during which I was informed I was "morbidly obese." This month, I'm going to ask you guys for your help, after I tell you what I see when I look in the toilet now that I'm on the fat-blocking pharmaceutical, Xenical.

What follows is not for the faint of heart, and I realize it has very little place in a borderline skin mag like *Arena*. So if you're easily grossed out and have zero interest in my bowel movements or my weight problem, I urge you to flip forward a few pages and check out whichever Brit chick is showing off her nearly-naked boobs this month.

They say that only a certain type of personality looks into the contents of the bowl before flushing. I fall into that group, because I never fail to take a look at what's passed out of me when I'm on the throne. As shitting is about the closest parallel to the birthing process that I can lay claim to (I don't count my screen-writing, as too many critics have likened my scripts to literal dumps for me to feel maternal toward my scrib-bling), I always take a gander at my "kids" before they head out to sea. I've earned that right as a "parent."

But since ingesting Xenical three times daily (once with each meal), I've been treated to a peek inside the digestive process heretofore afforded only the most hearty gastrointestinal parasites. There's a side effect of the drug that makes toilet time even messier than before, as you're no longer just wiping away the fecal matter that didn't go quietly into that good night and instead opted to cling to your ring; now, you're also *mopping up* Café Brown-Eye as well.

I'll let this passage from the handy-dandy leaflet

attached to the bottle of Xenical explain.

"Because Xenical works by blocking the absorption of dietary fat, it is likely that you will experience some changes in bowel habits. These generally occur during the first weeks of treatment; however they may continue throughout your use of Xenical. These changes may include oily spotting..."

AKA, peculiar orange stains in your underwear.

"...gas with discharge..."

AKA, you fart and *matter* accompanies the fumes.

"...urgent need to go to the bathroom..."

Because you don't want matter to accompany the fumes into your underwear when you fart anymore.

"...and oily, fatty stools."

Good fucking God, how horrible does that sound? Those are three words that should never be grouped together: oily, fatty stools. Doesn't it just conjure up the most hellish image in your mind's eye? When I read that, all I could see for days was a flabby, greasy turd chortling at me, shaking a fat finger in my general direction and reminding me that "You brought this on yourself, Fat Boy."

And I *did* bring it on myself. I've rested on my laurels my entire life, and now it's caught up to me, physically. I'm the kind of moron who doesn't overachieve like I should; I accomplish just enough to get by. I mean, look at the visuals in the films I've directed—with all due respect to the cinematographers who've had to endure my pedestrian craftsmanship, my oeuvre is one long resume of a lazy visual stylist at work. Sure, visually speaking, the films have been passable; the audience understands the thoughts or story points I'm trying to convey. But only *barely.* A true craftsman would be far more diligent in creating images that didn't just do the job, but also moved and transported the viewer into a world that doesn't quite exist.

And as in my work, so, too, in my health have I been satisfied to merely squeak by, because it always seemed like there'd be time to get in shape, sooner or later. I remember weighing one fifty at age fourteen, and having a far more athletic school-chum once offer the observation that my *calves* were bigger than his *thighs.* And I said to myself that, one day, I'd do something about that.

Just not today.

And before I knew it, "just not today" has turned into seventeen years of rather unhealthy living. I'd gone from being overweight to being "morbidly obese" (as opposed to "vitally obese"—a condition that doesn't get nearly as much ink, probably because it's right up there with another at-one-time-acceptable medical and social malady, "functioning alcoholism"). How could I face my friends, my parents, and even my wife, knowing that I was a ticking time bomb of blubbery self-indulgence?

Maybe in an *Arena* column?

No—it was that kind of laze that got me to the pill-popping point at which I found myself. If I was going to turn it all around, it had to start with me telling those nearest and dearest to me that I wasn't that far removed from a Homer Simpson–style muumuu.

I started with my wife. Granted, she may view me through love's eyes, but she's not blind; nobody takes up as much of the bed as I do and doesn't arouse health concerns in his significant other. When I related the doctor's warnings to her and told her about the prescription he insisted I take, she gave me a hug, told

me she'd help in any way I asked, and then took me to
bed. It was probably a ploy to take my mind off the fact
that I was really, really fat, but I didn't complain. I
mean, who am I all of a sudden that I'd be above a
mercy hump?

When I told my parents, my mother (a pharmaceutical genius in her own right, due to the wide array of
heart medication she takes to keep her ticker tocking)
and father seemed to brighten up considerably—as
they'd started wondering if they were going to outlive
their youngest son. Like my wife, they hugged me and
told me they'd help me in any way I asked, but thankfully, stopped short of taking me to bed. Don't get me
wrong, I'm all for a three-way; just not with my parents.

When I told my friends, they neither hugged me,
nor threw me a mercy hump—they were too fixated on
the oily, fatty stools. I told them that the blocked fat
that comes out with the rest of my waste looks a lot like
pizza grease when it drips off a hot slice onto a paper
plate. Needless to say, all concerns for my health took a
back seat to the sudden macabre interest in my poop.

But as I sat there day after day those first few weeks

of imbibing Xenical, going through rolls and rolls of toilet paper, trying to blot the oil from my ass after every squat, all I could think of was you, dear reader.

Follow me on this one: if I don't make this info public, I may backslide and do nothing about my weight, until suddenly, I'm twenty pounds heavier than I am *now*. The Xenical can only do so much (unless the desired result was to piss oil out of my ass with every pinched loaf; in which case, the Xenical sure has delivered in spades); the rest has to come from me. And since I'm a weak-willed cookie-inhaler, that means it's gotta come from you guys too.

While my relationship with those who watch the flicks I've been involved with is a warm one, there's always this element of the three-ton, giant pink elephant to our meet-and-greets; that is to say, nobody mentions the weight gain. Well, I'm saying it's okay to mention the weight-gain now. It *needs* attention called to it, to keep a brother ever-vigilant. Why the fuck else would I be writing about the nasty nature of my greasy ass-brownies in a magazine? I obviously can't police myself, so I'm looking to you folks for help.

So if you see me somewhere, and I'm tearing into food that no one over two hundred pounds should be enjoying, pop over, say hi, and then remind me that you never want to read about my oily, fatty stools again. Believe me—a comment like that'll straighten me right the fuck out, and I'll put the donut down and back away.

Homer weighed three hundred and fifteen pounds when he donned the muumuu.

I currently weigh two hundred and ninety-five—a mere twenty pounds from being a total cartoon.

I'd like to weigh two forty, max, and I don't want to go through a stomach-stapling to get there.

Help me before I eat myself to death.

Next month: a less oily and fatty column!

Spider-Man

THANK THE ALMIGHTY JESUS CHRIST that I'm married, because in this column, my inner movie/comic book nerd is going to take over and go *so* spastic over a fanboy flick that any chance of my ever landing a chick after this piece hits print will be about as strong as . . . as . . .

Well, as strong as Peter Parker *before* he got bit by the radioactive spider.

You hear that? That's the sound of thousands of distaff *Arena* readers turning the page.

But *fuck* girls! This summer, there's an event film gracing cinema screens that the sweaty subculture of geekdom has been awaiting like the second coming (or even the *first* cumming; at least the first cumming that's not all over their own hands; or the first cumming that's not shot into the business end of a petroleum jelly–smeared vacuum cleaner; or the first cumming that doesn't wind up inside the ass of the family dog). And being a proud, card-carrying member of that sexy, worldly set, I, too, have been (greasily) shitting myself in anticipation.

No, fellow no-lifers—I'm not talking about the theatrical debut of *Divine Secrets of the Ya-Ya Sisterhood*.

I'm talking about *Spider-Man*.

Now, being an American, we get all the good stuff first (with the exception of tea, Monty Python, civilization in general, international respect of our peers, Eddie Izzard, and a good look at Baby Rocco), so I've already seen the flick. And since I'm a big fan of the Britains (both of them), I'm going to spoil the hell out of this gargantuan title for you like a motherfucker.

When I first saw the *Spider-Man* movie, I hated it.

Really, really fucking hated it.

Like I-wanted-to-find-screenwriter-David-Koepp-and-bite-his-nuts-hard-between-my-own-heterosexual-teeth hated it.

But as much as I was pissed off at the filmmakers, the studio, and the world over this Spider-Turd, I uncharacteristically kept my mouth shut about it, the rationale being "This movie's gonna be huge regardless of how much it sucks, and if it's huge, there will be more comic book movies, and I want more comic book movies, so zip it." And as I'm usually about as discreet as a fart in a monastery, this took a great deal of strength on my part. So when asked at a college Q&A early in April if I'd seen the movie already, I replied, "I've seen *Spider-Man.*" When pressed for details in the way of *"And…"* I offered in return only, "I've seen *Spider-Man.*"

My initial *Spider* screening was at my house, courtesy of a good friend over at Columbia/Tristar who'd slipped me a copy of the flick long before it hit screens in May. Even though we've got a kick-ass surround-sound digital projection setup with the drop-down screen and whatnot, I limited the audience to me, my wife, and our friend Dan—figuring that having too many people see it for free before it opened might hurt the film's box office take (for the record, *Spider-Man* took in $114 million its opening weekend; I'd like to think that was largely because I kept my early screening to a mere three viewers).

For the first half hour, you couldn't Buffalo Bill that smile off my face, so obviously elated was I to be not only watching *Spider-Man*, but watching it well in advance of its theatrical release in the privacy of my own home. And worse, I was playing the part of the tour guide through the flick, hipping (and I use that term veeeery loosely) Jen and Dan to the ultimate fate of the characters' comic book counterparts.

"Young Harry Osborn later takes up his father's mantle as the Green Goblin!" I'd coo excitedly.

"Ooo! Mary Jane! The future Mrs. Peter Parker!" I'd beam dreamily.

And the whole time, my wife is casting dead glances at me that seem to say, "I can't believe I let someone as geeky as you put his cock in me."

But at about forty-five minutes into the movie, something seemed wrong. Gone was my smile. Long gone were the pronouncements of who'll later do what in the Spider-Man mythos. What I was left with was a sinking feeling that quickly evolved into deep disappointment and a bitchy filmmaker's catty take on what was fast shaping up to be just another very expensive, overblown piece-of-shit summer movie.

"Oh my God, the terrible dialogue!" I began muttering to myself. "All these scenes are ripped off from other, *better* comic book movies! And what's with the Green Goblin's fucking costume?"

Oh, that costume! Whose idea was it to take such an expressive actor as Willem Dafoe—he who so creepily brought to life Max Schreck in *Shadow of the Vampire* simply by sneering—and encase him in a metal shell and mask that make him resemble less a robot than a high-end dildo? Not seeing Spider-Man's facial expressions is something even the most comics-ignorant folks in the audience would expect, because Spider-Man's historically been visually represented as an expressionless bodysuit that makes quick quips. But not the Green Goblin! And not Willem Dafoe *playing* the Green Goblin! It was tantamount to putting Jack Nicholson in a Greek Tragedy mask as the Joker in *Batman*.

Everything I hated about *Spider-Man* culminated in one scene in the picture in which the equally fully masked Spider-Man and Green Goblin are having a stunningly banal conversation on a rooftop about whether they should be friends or enemies. The scene was so over-the-top bad that I was pulled completely out of the story and found myself wondering instead whether or not Tobey Maguire and Willem Dafoe were even *in* the costumes when the scene was shot. I swear, that moment in the film resembles a toy commercial, selling two inanimate action figures (which is kind of what the movie is anyway, but still); all that's missing are the nine- to thirteen-year-old hands holding both characters at the waist, slamming them into one another, with a voiceover assuring "Comes with every-thing you see here."

When the credits started rolling, Jen and Dan were merely bored, while I was livid. I'm not even the biggest Spider-Man fan on the planet (that title belongs to this sweaty, four hundred pound loss squeezed into a 4XL "Spidey Goes Cosmic" T-shirt I saw at a comic book convention once), but I felt betrayed.

Then, last week, I went to see *Spider-Man* in a movie theater. As much as I loathed it the first time, I figured I should at least see it on the big screen—the way Sam Raimi intended it to be seen. And since I'm a Sam Raimi fan (I mean, *Evil Dead 2* is beyond brilliant, and *A Simple Plan* may be one of the most watchable films ever made), I put my bias against the box office record-breaker that is *Spider-Man* in my back pocket, sucked it up, and subjected myself to a repeat viewing.

Since it was a matinee show about two weeks after the movie had opened, the theater wasn't very packed. I stuffed myself into a seat, crossed my arms, and prepared to bitterly hate the flick all over again.

But something weird happened.

There in the dark, side by side with about fifty other people (who apparently have as little to do as I during the day), against all my better judgement, I started to smile again. Suddenly, I was no longer listening to David Koepp's bad dialogue or obsessing over the stiffness of the Green Goblin's costume. I was watching the Spider-Man the character's creators, Stan Lee and Steve Ditko, must've envisioned when they sat down to create a legend all those years ago. I wasn't watching the movie as a filmmaker anymore, but as a movie buff—and one who loves comics as much as he loves . . . even more comics. And one by one, the prejudices born out of that video-projected screening in my home theater slipped away, and what I was left with was the sheer enjoyment of watching Peter Parker accept the fact that with great power must come great responsibility, and the infinite pleasure in seeing Spider-Man swing through the Manhattan skyline.

Sure, I've still got gripes with some of the elements of *Spider-Man;* shit, even someone who's so loyal to Spidey that they defend the "Clone Saga" has to agree that the rooftop scene was pretty bad. But at the end of the day, *Spider-Man* works on that primal level we're always seeking to get back to when we fork over a small fortune at the ticket window: the simple awe at watching a hero come to life before your eyes. And if you let it, the movie'll make you feel like a kid again.

At least by the second viewing.

Now *Episode II: Attack of the Clones*? I didn't even need to see the whole movie all the way through—let alone twice—to know they got *that* flick right.

All I had to see was Yoda toss aside his cane and reach for his lightsaber, and it was just like busting a nut in the family dog all over again.

Um...

Westward, Ho!

ONE OF THE BEST/WORST THINGS about being in the movie biz is the inside poop you get on the stars who shell out so much of their multimillions to spin doctors and flacks whose sole reason for being is to keep their clients' images squeaky clean and far from scandal, so that audiences will continue to drive the box office of their movies (not to mention their ever-increasing paychecks) toward figures so high that they rival the entire fiscal budget of the state of Rhode Island, if not New Jersey. The moment you get your foot into Tinsel Town's door, you're informed of all manner of movie-star debauchery that makes the tabloid stuff seem church bulletin-ish in comparison.

For example, in the last week alone, I've been

tipped off by several credible sources that the up-and-coming (some would say, already there) macho action star who looks like he's all about the pussy is apparently really, really gay. In the constantly shifting terrain of sexual identity that even non-Hollywood America finds itself grappling with, though, that's hardly shocking. Surprising, yes—considering this is a guy who's probably got every fifteen to twenty-year-old girl (hell, even their mothers) salivating over the thought of having the dude's huge biceps crushing their midriffs as he works their nipples while going down on them. But shocking? C'mon—cock-chugging (either by men or women) is a Hollywood standard, really. Just as when you go to Philadelphia, you're supposed to at least *try* a cheesesteak sandwich, when you arrive in Los Angeles, you're almost *expected* to sample a stiff one in the mouth.

For shocking, you have to go to the *really* unpleasant bit of info I was fed recently (which so filled me up, I was able to pass on the stiff one altogether), regarding one of this country's greatest living actors. Word on the street is he likes to lie under glass tables and watch women pinch out loaves while he jerks off. That, as they say, takes the cake. Or the brownie, in this case.

What is it about Hollywood that brings out the Salo in the rich and famous? Largely, this is the kind of behavior that you only hear about actors, not actresses, partaking in. And in the bizarrely backwards politically correct atmosphere of the early twenty-first century, I know you're supposed to credit women with being *just* as perverse and sexually deviant as men, but let's face it—not only are actresses too busy vomiting up every meal, stapling their stomachs shut, and having the top five layers of their skin acid-burned off to maintain some semblance of their youthful appearance, but also women are generally far too sensible to be even remotely curious about what it looks like at the exhaust end of some dude when he opens up his brown eye and dirty-winks at them.

So it's the insanely successful *actors* who have the most outlandish kinks, and one can only wonder how they find themselves so sexually jaded that only a Stinkin'-Log will help them raise the barn. Is it that when you're able to fuck and suck every gorgeous woman on the planet, it gets a little old? Is it kind of like being fed every type of succulently prepared entree, handcrafted by the world's finest chefs, for a year straight, and then growing so weary of it that suddenly, you feel compelled to see what dog food tastes like? Is the culture of celebrity so permissive that even fecal antics aren't really pushing the edge of the envelope anymore? And what's the next step toward the carnal abyss for these guys, most of them husbands and even fathers? Cat asses? Corpse fucking? Jerking off to mid–plastic surgery images of Joan Rivers?

These were the questions I asked myself before I decided to move to Hollywood.

As of January of this year, I packed up the family and headed west, which is something I never … NEVER … thought I'd do. I was born and raised in New Jersey, and have been able to stay there through the first (and probably final, once this nearly name-dropping piece of career suicide makes the rounds of the Cigarette Smoking Man–like cabals that actually run the movie biz) eight years of my filmmaking career. It's always been a point of pride with me. Moving to California once they got their foot in the door of the movie biz was something lesser men (and women) with flexible integrity did, not me. Making my home in Los Angeles would be akin to selling out.

But let's not pull punches here: I sold out a *long* time ago. My career's been bought and paid for five times over, because I've accepted (and, oftentimes, begged for) money from studios to finance my celluloid whimsies. For years now, the shorthand used to describe me by a press corps that couldn't be bothered to figure out another label to slug before my name has been "indie filmmaker Kevin Smith." But, in truth, I haven't been an indie since the first two weeks of '94. The moment Miramax bought *Clerks* at the Sundance Film Festival, the "indie" title became negligible, as they, in turn, are owned by Walt Disney (the monolithic corporation, not the cryogenically frozen Mouse-maker himself). When Universal put up the six million bucks for me to make *Mallrats,* my sellout hymen was busted beyond repair and I was no longer "cherry." *Chasing Amy, Dogma, Jay and Silent Bob Strike Back*—all of these were financed by Miramax coin, which in turn was probably earned off your backs, gentle readers, if you've ever taken a trip to Disney World and paid five bucks for an ice cream bar shaped like Mickey's face.

No, the only reason the press (and, by extension, the folks who read and believe the press *that* press presses) still maintain I'm an indie filmmaker is because they find the shit we've shot hard to categorize (as opposed to the shit the actor guy is rumored to like getting a peep at shooting out the ass of chicks who I can only assume have a total lack of self-consciousness). "Cult Filmmaker" would probably be a more apt label. "Lucky Sumbitch Who Keeps Failing Upwards Filmmaker" would be even better. But no matter how many times I'll tell folks "The only truly independent film I've ever made was *Clerks*," I've long since accepted the fact that if I'm seventy-five, and I've just directed *Clerks Part VIII: A Flat-Out Commercial for Coca-Cola, Nike, and McDonald's* for DisneyCo., starring a cast of whichever hot, young actors are on the nation's number-one TV show at the time, the press will still call me "Indie Filmmaker Kevin Smith."

So, old sellout that I am, I couldn't really argue

against moving to Los Angeles anymore. And honestly, I didn't want to, after spending a year out here making *Jay and Silent Bob Strike Back.* You spend a year any- where (well, maybe not prison or Calcutta) with your family, and it becomes home, really. Because the old adage is true: home *is* where your heart's at. And my heart's at the feet of my wife and kid.

Jen never liked New Jersey. Raised in Florida, and a Los Angeles resident for seven years before we met, the notion of a state that has actual shifting weather pat- terns never appealed to her. She has a seventy-degree mentality. That's how I'm cocksure my wife loves me— not because she gave up her writing gig at *USA Today* and moved to New Jersey to be with me after we fell in love, but solely because she moved to New Jersey at *all,* not to mention stayed there, for four years. Lest you think her a real martyr, let me assure you that during those four years she never missed an opportunity to remind me how much she *hated* living there. Jen would find one small way every day to let me know there was a better place to live than where we were. That was her retribution for being made to suffer through freezing, blizzard-condition winters and humid, mosquito-plagued summers. And every time she lamented about how much better off we'd be in Los Angeles, I'd lash out at her, "Hey, man—don't try to change me! I'm an indie filmmaker!"

Yeah—even *I* buy into the label sometimes.

But it wasn't the power of my wife (who, honestly, has me so wrapped around her finger that she could probably—in very few words—convince me to watch her fuck three of my worst enemies in our bed while I stood naked in a corner of the bedroom, reading aloud from the most damning and dismissive reviews any of the flicks I've made have ever received, while *The Brothers McMullen* played on the TV in the background) and her never-ending, none-too-subtle suggestions to pack up and head west that finally made me pull up the Garden State stakes.

It was the kid.

When you've got a kid, you want them to enjoy their childhood—mainly so that they don't blow all your cash on therapists down the line, bitching about how miserable you made them in their youth. I figure my kid's already got a few years of couch trips ahead of her, coming to grips with the fact that she's the daughter of "Silent Bob"—a point that's kind of embarrassing already, and will only grow more so the further we move away from those movies, and the audience starts to wonder "What the fuck were we laughing at anyway?" Why compound that by adding injury to insult in ruining her childhood? And the easiest way to ruin any kid's childhood? You show them what life is like when they can go outside and swim in the pool and run around in the yard every day of the year because the weather's always a mild seventy-two degrees, then yank that shit out from under them by dragging their confused asses back to a place where the pool's got a cover bolted over it nine months out of the year, and they can't even get outside to grab a lungful of fresh air because the snow's piled so high against the door that you're looking at your flesh and blood, wondering what part of their body you're going to have to eat first to stay alive once the rations run out.

After being in Los Angeles for a year, my daughter Harley became a real outdoorsy kid. Me, I was never one of those—which is probably why I always look like I *have* already eaten several family members to stay alive, snow or no snow. And being that Harley has what appears to be my very dominant genes coursing through her tiny frame, her life's going to be an uphill battle to *not* look like me as she gets older. And I'm not even talking about the beard here; this kid's got a pair of legs and an ass on her that my wife's always saying looks "real familiar." If the Lord answers my prayers, Harley will chrysalis during puberty into a tall, shapely woman who more resembles her mother; but for the moment, she looks like a miniature, nonsmoking version of her dad. And if she were to live a life that kept her housebound in front of the TV for three-quarters of the year, we might as well get her a sleeveless, hooded sweatshirt and a prescription for Xenical *now;* because with my cursed DNA torpedoing her at this early stage of the game, the forecast for her future aesthetic is looking pretty grim. Having grown up a fat kid, I don't wish that on anybody, let alone someone I love so much. As unfair as it is, this is a thin man's (and thinner woman's) world; as such, I want Harley to have the best chance she can get to triumph in that same war against the scale I've waged for most of my life.

And who wound up being her hero in what will become that never-ending battle? The same guy who's saved the world three times over now.

Once from an asteroid the size of Texas.

Once from a sewer monster.

And once again, this summer, in *The Sum of All Fears.*

She calls him Uncle Ben.

An Interview with Ben Affleck

I'VE READ JUST ABOUT every Ben Affleck article that's been published since *Good Will Hunting* heralded the arrival of a guy *People* magazine recently dubbed "The Sexiest Man Alive." I'd be dishonest if I didn't cop to doing this because I'm a press-whore who likes to see his name in ink and, eight times out of ten, when Ben's interviewed, you can usually find some backhanded compliment for me included in the text, corroborating the author's contention that he's a good guy/good actor.

But I don't read profiles on Affleck solely because I'm a big fan of me. I do it because I'm actually a bigger fan of him. This shouldn't come as much of a surprise to anyone who's seen my last four films or might see the next one, due out sometime this year, called *Jersey Girl*. I'm a firm believer in Affleck, the Actor. In my estimation, Affleck is right for almost every role. Trying to fly a new *Superman* flick? Cast Affleck. Someone wants to essay the life of Christ yet again? Affleck's your savior. They're making another *Jaws*? Affleck can play the shark.

But as much as I'm an Affleck-as-Actor booster (not to mention an Affleck-as-Writer booster as well; *Good Will Hunting* is one of the few films in recent memory that actually deserved its Best Screenplay Academy Award win), I'm probably an even bigger fan of Affleck, the friend. Which means this piece will be about as controversial as a third-grade valentine. Anyone looking for some muckraking, raised-eyebrow, "Can Affleck Make *Daredevil* Swing Like *Spider-Man*, Or Is He Just Another Jackass In Tights?" type of article is in for a letdown.

Anyone looking for a story that opens with Affleck's childhood predilection for porn, however, has just hit the jackpot.

"In my day, we had to steal porn from our dad's lockboxes," says Benjamin Geza, sprawled out on a couch in a Hollywood Hills house that used to be his but is now mine. The well-below-market price he generously gave it to me for further guarantees only softballs in this interview. "This dude used to have this garage, this storage barn in the backyard. And three of us broke in one day and found this stash of *Penthouse* and *Playboy*. That was the motherlode to us. Oh, God, it was almost too much. It was like crack, you know what I mean? All of us were in the bathroom for weeks."

Lest women everywhere find themselves clutching at their clits, rapt by the fantasy of the Ben Affleck they all know and love gently throttling his cock in a greased-up, slow-mo, Candida Royale–porn style, that's the pre-pubescent Jack Ryan engaged in some hormonally-induced, adolescent, Bostonian breaking and entering. Before you can play a character bent on justice, you've gotta bend a few laws yourself, I guess.

But Affleck's made an art form of breaking laws, mostly the laws of averages. By age thirty, he's head-lined a dozen movies, taken his salary into the eight-figure range, and scored the aforementioned Oscar. And he'll break the law yet again this month, as he goes against all common Hollywood wisdom by covering up his multimillion dollar mug with a horned mask, playing the titular role in *Daredevil*. The Marvel Comics second-stringer, barely known outside of comic book stores, is poised to make the jump to the big leagues, standing on the shoulders of Mister *Pearl Harbor*.

Created by Stan Lee and Bill Everett, Daredevil has always been the Grateful Dead to Spider-Man's Rolling Stones—the lesser-known yet ardently adored of the Marvel spandex set. As a child, Matt Murdock lost his sight to a radioactive isotope, only to have his remaining senses heightened to superhuman degrees (he can track a bad guy by listening for signature heartbeats, he can "read" a newspaper by running his fingertips over the ever-so-slightly-raised ink). Later in life, the blind lawyer takes to leaping off the rooftops of Hell's Kitchen, and beating the shit out of muggers, adorned in a red jumpsuit. Affleck may have earned his reported twelve-million-dollar salary for the balls it took to pour himself into crimson leather alone.

"I think it's better than the Batsuit." The man who's cinematically saved the world from meteors, nuclear mishaps, and a sewer monster nods. "I heard a lot of bitching in the press about the Batsuit from various *Batman* actors. I think because it was latex, it was restrictive, where the cowl was stuck to the shoulders. But the Daredevil costume is like a motorcycle racing outfit—tight leather jacket, tight leather pants and then, like, this armor, padding stuff. The argument was that it was utilitarian. He wears it because it protects him from the blows."

No stranger to blows himself, Affleck has had to contend with the vocal minority on the Internet that hasn't been shy about chiming in with their displeasure over his casting, calling to mind the howls of cacophonous derision heard over ten years ago, when Tim Burton announced that Michael Keaton would don Batman's cape and cowl. Most will recall, however, the satisfied silence Keaton's actual performance was met with, as that 1989 flick went on to gross over two hundred million bucks.

"I really don't know what they're saying about *Daredevil* on the Internet," confesses Ben, chowing down on yet another piece of Nicorette in an effort to wean himself off his pack-a-day smoking habit. "My understanding is the fans like the trailer, the fans like the suit. And I would think they would, as comic book fans, because it's just like the comic. I don't go to these sites, though, because there's always going to be somebody with some biased criticism. You never get to a point in your life where there's not some guy waiting to say 'Fuck your bullshit.' You can't please everybody, not everybody is going to like you. The thing about this business is it's the business of long, sharp knives, you know what I mean? And so by its very nature, the Internet is like a dog market, and when the barking stops, you realize that all that noise was over a movie, and what was the point? Movies are just kind of binary in a weird way—like they either kind of work or they don't. You can dress up a piece of shit, and you can do a lot to chip away at something that is golden, but at some level, the thumbs-up, thumbs-down thing is oftentimes a fairly true barometer."

This type of pragmatism is the hallmark of the Ben Affleck I grew to love many years ago, before the lesbian pictures, the Jack Ryan mantle inheritances, the quiet, subtle, press-shy relationship with Jennifer Lopez.

Affleck was a guy I first read about in *Variety* a day before he came in to audition for that cinematic blockbuster *Mallrats.* There was a notice about his and actor friend Matt Damon's sale of the *Good Will Hunting* script to Castle Rock, for a handsome six-figure sum (years later, we brought the script to Miramax in turnaround). I remember being impressed with the Sisters-Are-Doing-It-For-Themselves attitude: rather than be content to bitch about the paucity of work for relative unknowns, a pair of actors, so hungry for not just good roles, but *any* roles, wrote their own script, and wound up selling it with themselves attached to star. I dug that. Self-starters get me all wet. So when this actor-turned-writer even bothered to show up for his audition in my little dick-and-fart-joke opus, I was a bit taken aback. Had it been me, I probably would've said "Screw your mall picture—I'm a writer now too, bee-yotch!" Yet there he was, still pounding the pavement, hat in hand.

But the humility didn't stop there. The nature of his role in *Rats* being somewhat small, Ben asked if he could head back to L.A. from our Minnesota set whenever he wasn't shooting, so he could work through the copious notes Castle Rock was trying to ruin *Good Will* with. I happily obliged, as one less actor hanging around the set could never be considered a bad thing. And then, Affleck did something that forever endeared him to me: whenever he would leave for a few days, he'd write me what was essentially a thank-you note.

"Thanks for not only casting me, but also letting me go work on the script back home," the first of these not-very-Virginia-Woolf notes read. "I'm having a great time on the flick, and I think it's shaping up to be some funny shit."

It's rare when someone puts pen to paper anymore, and rarer still when an actor thinks about someone other than himself. That simple gesture kicked off a friendship that's lasted nearly ten years, during which time I've watched that humble note-writer blossom into a humble, bona fide movie star.

"It's fun to be in a movie where they—I don't know if this is a real verb, but it's become one in Hollywood—'event-ize' the picture," he observes of the full-court push Twentieth Century Fox is giving the Mark Stephen

Johnson–directed *Daredevil*. "It doesn't necessarily mean that it's going to be a hit, or whatever—obviously you never know. But because it's a superhero movie, and superhero movies are so popular now, or at least *Spider-Man* was, the studio's going out of their way to promote it. You know, it feels a little bit more standout. Which is good and bad I guess."

Standing out is something Ben's always done fairly well. Blessed with stunning good looks and a matinee idol's chin, he could've chosen to skate through life as nothing more than a pretty boy. But ever the over-achiever, the son of English teacher Chris sports a vocabulary far more expansive than the usual marquee actor's, and his almost encyclopedic knowledge of history, politics, religion, current events, and, yes, the movie biz elevates him beyond simple boy-toy into very nearly Übermensch territory—thus ruining the grade curve for the rest of us shlubs.

Jennifer Lopez recognized this, and recently took Benny from the Block off the market. The pair met while shooting this summer's *Gigli* and coupled up a few months later. By the time we started rehearsing

Jersey Girl, in which Ben and Jen again costar, love was in full bloom. By the second day of rehearsal, he pulled me aside to ask what I thought of his girlfriend. As it was more than apparent that this was not merely his latest conquest but the love of his life, I told him, "I bet you're married within a year."

"You think?" he asked, coyly, already probably sure himself.

But I didn't *think*; I *knew*. And so did he—as, about halfway through the shoot, a smiling-ear-to-ear Lopez extended her hand to me, to vogue the three-million-dollar Harry Winston pink diamond Ben had secretly given her a week before. After a few seconds, I realized it was on *that* finger. The thunderous sonic boom heard later that month was the sound of millions of hearts, both male and female, breaking in unison, when the celebs went public with the news of their engagement. It'll be his first marriage, and her third—which has prompted nearly everyone I've met over the course of the last half year to quiz me about whether the relationship is authentic or just a publicity stunt.

Ever the diplomat, Affleck doesn't bristle at the blatant cynicism total strangers project toward his personal life.

"I think that's got to be a product of the fact that it got so much publicity," he offers, reflecting on the media feeding frenzy that surrounded the news of his impending nuptials. "But to think it's a publicity stunt... *c'mon.* I mean, if it was, it'd be bad timing. You'd want to get all that press when either *Gigli* or *Jersey Girl* was coming out, not months away from release. Besides—movies fronted by people who are married historically haven't done so well. It may take a minimum of ten years of marriage and a couple kids, but sooner or later, people will get that we're in love."

How can he be so zen about the intense scrutiny the media has placed his relationship under? Simple: neither he nor his intended pick up gossip mags or turn on *Entertainment Tonight* anymore. Who has the spare time? As Ben points out, with a smile, "I'm busy having sex with my future wife."

The man's got a point—would you give a shit what people were saying about you in the disposable tabloid press if you were fucking Jennifer Lopez? Or Ben Affleck, for that matter?

Whether anyone wants to see a married-with-children Ben Affleck picture, Ben Affleck wants to live a married-with-children life. On the set of *Jersey Girl*, between takes, Affleck could always be found cuddling his infant costars. He was fearless in a way most men aren't with other people's kids. When presented with someone else's baby, I can usually be found dashing to the furthest corner of the room, so as not to be the guy who drops the baby. On the opposite end of the spectrum, Affleck not only gleefully accepted any infant thrown at him, it was hard to get him to give the kids back.

"I didn't think about the dropping thing too much," he chuckles. "They're pretty sturdy, aren't they? You've just got to cradle them. I loved them, particularly the little ones. I was fascinated by how tiny they are, like a different species, and how they eventually end up as real people. Over time, these little fingers grow out, and either change the world or clutch a crack pipe. But I'd like to have a few of them. I don't know how Jen is on it. Women, they're the ones who have to do the lion's share of the work. Conception I'm all up for, ready to go. And I'll be there during the birth. I'll root! I'll cheer! You do it! Go! Push! And she'll be like, maybe number eight is enough, Ben."

If the future Affleck/Lopez brood doesn't quite reach eight strong, it certainly won't be from lack of trying. There's no shortage of paparazzi-lensed pics of Bennifer, as I've taken to calling them, openly canoodling. Rather than live a life spent dodging shutterbugs, they've opted to simply be themselves publicly, press be damned.

"My feeling is I'm not going to change what I do because of the work that I do or because of the press or whatever. I'm not going to alter my life. I'm going to do what I'm going to do. After September 11 I was a little freaked out, and I was talking to a therapist, who said, 'I don't know about you, but if I have something to do, I'm gonna do it.' It's a simple philosophy, but I kind of live by it now. You can really waste a lot of time and a lot of life worrying about all the bad things that could happen, and I think as an actor you learn to take risks pretty early anyway. So we just decided to be ourselves

out there. The press can be daunting, but it just means
that you stay a little more aware of everything you're
doing in public, because you can kind of imagine it as a
tearout in *US Weekly*. It's like a bigger version of 'wear
clean underwear because you might be in a car acci-
dent.' But I don't sweat all that, because, ultimately, I've
got very little to complain about. I know I'm very lucky,
just to be able to be in a nice place in life, and do what I
love, and have somebody I love to share my life with.
That's pretty spectacular."

We're conducting this interview during an ultra-
rare moment of downtime in the ever-busy Affleck's
schedule. Last year he did three movies, back-to-back
(*Gigli, Daredevil,* and *Jersey Girl*). This year will see him
doing, at minimum, two (*Surviving Christmas* and
John Woo's *Paycheck*). It's a significant slowdown for a
guy who multitasks better than Macintosh OS X. The
thirty-year-old is finally learning to afford himself a day
or two off for good behavior. But how is he filling up
this vacation week?

"A lot of it is promotional stuff. I try to be with Jen
in the morning if I can, have a little dinner with friends,

go to a screening, sleep in a little bit, try to get my dogs out. There's usually stuff that comes up on the phone or a lot of e-mails. I'm on the computer a bunch or taking pictures, stuff like that. This week, a lot of Christmas shopping."

Even Ben's trips to the mall have become newsworthy, as reports of him and his betrothed dropping hundreds of thousands of dollars on one another clog the wire services. In this frightening new age when the world should be obsessing over the next terrorist attack, thank God we have Bennifer's shopping sprees to preoccupy us.

"She likes to go shopping, what can I say? And I don't mind buying gifts."

Indeed, one Christmas, five heavy boxes arrived at my office, with a note reading "You can't subsist on four-letter words alone, you undereducated fuck. Merry Christmas." He'd sent me the twenty-volume Oxford English Dictionary. This Christmas, the wife and I unwrapped a sterling silver cigarette case with matching lighter. The card read "To the last smokers on earth. Love, Ben and Jen."

Try to picture two of the most famous people in the universe bargain hunting in a department store and you might get an idea of how difficult it is for Bennifer to lead a normal life. The amount of time they spend stopping to sign autographs for flabbergasted passersby must cut the actual shopping time down by two-thirds. Never ones to turn away fans, I've watched both of them wade into a crowd of four hundred well-wishers outside of a shooting location, to sign anything they were presented with, displaying little regard for their safety.

"Well, they were all little girls," Affleck says, shrugging off the gutsy act. "There's not much to be gained by the assassination of me. It's not like I'm the king, or somebody who's trying to set back civil rights. But I feel like there's like certain compunction to sign autographs, if people show up or ask. They're fans. I'm generally pretty good, but I'm not a woman. I think it's harder for women, which is why it's good for Jen to have a bodyguard when she's out there doing the same. There can be a weird, leery, sexual predatory energy sometimes. With me, the worst it gets is someone call-

ing out 'Well fuck you!' from across the way, if I didn't
get to sign something for them."

Unwrapping his third piece of Nicorette, I ask him
why the sudden urge to stop the lone addiction he's
afforded himself, after quickly kicking an overpubli-
cized and overstated brief battle with the bottle back in
the summer of 2001.

"After a while you start to feel lazier and more
down, and you feel it in your lungs. I'm trying to break
the habit of smoking all the time that I associate with
reading, working on the computer, that whole thing. I
just think, what kind of an idiot will I be, having a heart
attack at fifty, or fucking cancer at forty-one? That
would mean that my life would end ten years from
now, eleven years from now. I would like to have more
time than that if I can help it."

Horseshit. His lady doesn't like it.

"That too," he concedes, caught. "Although if I did
get something terminal, I'd take it up to two, three
packs a day."

Lung cancer or not, the older Ben Affleck will more
than likely be as suited to run a movie studio as he'll be

to front their pictures. A true student of the business, I've always felt Ben would be as successful behind the cameras as he's been in front of them.

"I don't know if I'd want to throw my name in the hat for a studio head job, because as they exist now, unfortunately, studio heads have been pushed down the chain of command, due to these corporate hierarchies based on acquisitions. I don't know that I would like to have the responsibilities of having to report upward, of having to explain to a company that makes something else entirely, other than movies, why this is a good project or why that's a good project. The film business has gotten so vertically integrated, and the process of trying to translate creative instincts into pie charts and projected earnings is something I don't think anybody has fun with. It means you have to be even braver to make movies these days. People bad-mouth studio execs, but everybody thinks they know how to do it when they're not actually putting themselves on the line, having to decide 'Right, I've got to pick eight movies. If it's a disaster, I'm out of a job.' The problem with this business is that there's a lot of pseudoscience to it, but the ugly truth is that, to paraphrase William Goldman, nobody knows anything.

"I think Joe Roth [the head of Revolution Studios] has a pretty good setup. He's got very low overhead, he gets to do his movies, Sony picks up the marketing on them and takes a distribution fee, and sometimes, he directs. That's someone whose job I'd love to have. You know, to be able to write and direct and still foster the careers of other filmmakers and support them and go out and make these unusual movies as well as the more conventional movies. And Harvey [Weinstein, the cochairman of Miramax Films] does an interesting thing, where he works off Disney's money, but he has autonomy in what he can make."

So with studio boss out of the running, will Ben just continue to strap himself into red leather or play Tom Clancy's proxy in his golden years?

"I'd like to continue acting forever, but do like a Sidney Pollack, y'know?" Pollack, the director, costarred with (and nearly stole the show from) Affleck in last year's *Changing Lanes*. "Where you just kind of roll in, you don't do the junket, you do a phenomenal piece of character acting, and then you're out. The kind of acting I'm doing now, where you have to promote the movie by putting yourself out in front—it means all this stuff in your personal life is on display. It just starts to mess with your quality of life a little bit. Sometimes, it doesn't make me quite as happy as I thought it would."

But wait a second—if this guy bows out, who the hell's going to take up the mantle of Generation X's Harrison Ford? Aside from the obvious association with having assumed duties as Jack Ryan, Affleck stands at the threshold of Ford-dom in another significant fashion: if *Daredevil* works, he'll be an actor capable of carrying multiple franchises at once.

"Obviously that's an incredibly flattering comparison." He smiles, modestly. "But it's a little soon, knock wood, to say that *Daredevil* will work. Right now these superhero movies seem to be taking off, and the studios are franchising the ones that do well. *Spider-Man* is getting a sequel, *X-Men*, *Blade*, *Superman*, *Batman*. Hopefully, that'll be the case with this movie, because I'd love to keep playing Matt Murdock. I'd love to do the story you wrote as the next movie," he adds, referring to the *Daredevil* arc I wrote for Marvel Comics back in '99. "I think that might even be a better storyline to do than this first movie. It'd be fun. I think the trick about franchising is to make the movies better the second time out. You know—*refine* them. I like to say the only sequels that were better than the originals were *Huckleberry Finn, The Godfather: Part II,* and the New Testament.

"But it's a wonderful place to be in right now, with *Daredevil,* and I'm excited at the prospect of this movie working. I hope people respond to it, because it's faithful to the comic books, which I really love. It's as faithful to the source as any comic book adaptation has been."

And while it's going to be enjoyable watching Ben play the hero, during production on *Jersey Girl* I got to witness a true display of gallantry on his part, not to mention a secret identity of sorts.

We were shooting in a restaurant full of three hundred extras at the Philadelphia chapter of the Hard Rock Café, and at one point between takes, I see Affleck scoop a kid up out of a wheelchair and carry him over to the monitors for a better view of the scene. Later, I was introduced to the kid in question: Joe Kindregan, a thirteen-year-old stricken with AT, an extremely rare disease affecting maybe only fifty people, that Affleck describes as "like having cancer, AIDS, and MS all rolled into one."

Joe, whose speech is severely affected by his condition, is a regular on the set of every Affleck picture since the two met on *Forces of Nature*. Ben's become close with Joe's family, and hosts them not only on shoots, but also at his premieres. Affleck even spoke before Congress on the subject of stem cell research, and its potential benefits in the treatment of AT victims.

Joe's mother Suzie showed me a photo album she's been keeping of Ben's involvement with their life, a sort of *Ben and Joe's Excellent Adventures.* Here's two pages of pics of the Kindregans with Ben at the *Pearl Harbor* premiere in Hawaii. Here's another page of them at the *Sum of All Fears* premiere in Washington. Here's a group shot of Ben, Matt Damon, Joe and family at a Flyers game. I started to well up, struck by the notion that I know nothing about my friend's secret identity as a hero to a very sick little boy. As much as I'd always thought the world of Affleck, my affection and admiration for him instantly tripled.

"I try not to draw attention to it," Ben admits, obviously uncomfortable talking about it with a tape recorder running. "For the most part I'm a man who believes in knowing his scripture. Matthew, chapter 6, verse 2—pray in the closet instead of praying in the streets. Do your charity in private because it's something of a betrayal when you hustle and tell everybody what a great guy you are. I think there's something more enriching about doing it for its own sake, you know what I mean? And also, the truth is, I like the family. They're nice. It's not a great sacrifice for me; it's like, come on down, to D.C. or whatever. It's a couple of days out of my life. And I think he's a great kid. We've become good friends. His speech has gotten much worse, but he writes e-mails pretty well still.

"And I get something out of it, too. I get to feel like I'm contributing—particularly because I work in a profession that seems really vacuous and empty. I'm certainly not the most charitable guy; I'm not Mother

Teresa, but I try to do little things to contribute in some way. That's why I think people should give money anonymously, because it's really suspect when it's like 'Look at me! I'm a good man!'

"Robin showed me that," Affleck says, referring to his *Good Will* costar Robin Williams. "He goes to hospitals anonymously, every now and again, never bringing press, and does stand-up for kids with terminal illnesses. And I just thought that was cool, him just showing up like that. And I could see it meant as much to him as it did to the kids. And he didn't want anyone to know about it, he didn't want to bring cameras, he just wanted to go in and do his routines, and entertain the kids. Some of them knew who he was, and some of them thought he was just this lunatic. But it taught me that you could do something worthwhile with the celebrity the media affords you. It's kind of like taking what's normally a negative and spinning it into something worthwhile."

This is a far cry from the guy I've mercilessly mocked for being the most self-involved actor I've ever met (one of my Affleck routines involves him showing up for his dailies on every movie with a big bowl of popcorn, and sitting in the front row, audibly enjoying his performance aloud). Gone is Ben Affleck, playboy scamp. This is now a kinder, gentler Affleck. This is a motherfucker with severe nesting instincts, his biological clock ticking pretty loudly. Ben agrees.

"I just value different things now," he says, cracking open another Nicorette. "We're both in a different place than when we first met. These are our true formative years. I think we both have gone through a lot of stuff and seen a lot of different things. You know, this business is not new to us anymore, and also, we've started to realize that it doesn't fill your whole life, that it can't, that there's other stuff. And, in fact, living that stuff makes you a more interesting artist and storyteller and creative person because you have something personal to say. And yeah, it's nice. That's why I like working with you—because it's fun to work with your friends, people that you understand, get, and who really get you and get your back.

"I'm happiest working when I can find ways to make my professional life convergent with my personal life—so that going to work is an opportunity to hang out with the people you like as opposed to just feeling like work. Sometimes when you're as busy as you and I are, the few times we get to see each other over long periods of time is when we work together, which is fabulous."

Granted, this isn't really an interview, it's a mutual lovefest. But that's what you get when you send a friend to interview a friend. And that's what Ben is to me—a really good friend. I admire his talent and I cheer on his successes, but mostly, I rib him as much as I can—solely to mask what would be more or less rightly construed as an almost homoerotic blind allegiance. To a slew of bitter fucks, Ben Affleck may be a dick who hit the lottery of life many times over, but to me, he's the guy who took the time to write a few thank you notes, years back. And for that, and for the guy he's always been, and the admirable man he's shaping up to be, I'll always love him.

I recall when he wrapped on *Rats,* Ben asked, "You going to L.A. to edit this piece of shit?"

"Yeah, I'll be there all summer, trying to correct your terrible performance," I joked.

"Well when you get to town, you should call me," he'd said. And then, with an almost pathetic puppy-dog expression, he added this simple afterthought—the most sincere and accurate thing I've ever heard him utter.

"We should hang out. I'm a good guy."

He was, then. He still is, to this day.

Mulholland Drive

BEING THAT I LIVE, not on the cutting edge, but instead, on a dulled butter knife, I only recently got around to watching David Lynch's latest crusade into weirdness, *Mulholland Drive.*

Without ruining the flick for those of you who haven't peeped it yet, it's a story about obsession, regret, and how self-perception is a delicate tether that keeps us grounded in reality. Or at least, that's what my wife *told me* it was about—because when the credits started rolling, I didn't get that *at all.* At that point, I was just lost; very, very lost. And as I fancy myself a pretty smart cookie, when faced with my inability to process any film that doesn't conform to the somewhat identifiable standards of storytelling that were pounded

into me waaaaay back in grade school, rather than simply confess to my ignorance, I opted for the coward's
way out.

"That was fucking stupid," I offered, with all the
dismissive and authoritative tact I've become accus-
tomed to being at the receiving end of, courtesy of the
armchair-Eberts and pseudo-Siskels on the Internet
who feel the need to shit on *my* cinematic parade (and
yes—I know that analogy doesn't quite work anymore,
due to the fact that Gene Siskel was prematurely taken
from us a few years ago, and that if I wanted to make a
pop-culture reference that was less dated, I'd acknowl-
edge that there's a new guy, name of Roeper, sitting
across the aisle from Roger; but fuck Roeper—he ain't
now, nor will he ever be, the Mighty Gene, so he gets no
play in my literary tract; that, plus, alliteratively, Siskel's
name worked better).

"It made no *sense,*" I whined. "Fucking Lynch, I
swear. He's coasting. He's just being weird for the *sake*
of being weird now. He's become a parody of himself,
shitting out intentionally wacky crap because that's
what he's known for. What a letdown."

For the record, that's not nearly as harsh as I've gotten it from the eight fourteen-year-olds who populate the Internet.

So there I sat, on the bed, waiting for my wife to echo my sentiments, thus alleviating the nagging self-doubt I was suppressing by jizzing all over someone else's art rather than simply admitting to being too ignorant to understand it. But my wife, eyes glued on the credits, came back with "I thought it was awesome."

"Awesome? What the fuck are you talking about? It made no sense. It was a failed TV pilot that a network rejected, and all Lynch did was throw some tits into it, along with an incomprehensible wrap-up, so that all the yahoos at Cannes would nod approvingly and call him a genius yet again."

"I think it's brilliant," Jen offered.

"Good Lord, are you high? What's so brilliant about it? Enlighten me."

And she did.

"The blonde was so in love with the brunette that she went crazy after the brunette rejected her. The blonde had the brunette killed, but then couldn't live

with what she'd done, so she killed *herself.* The first
three quarters of the movie is her feverish, pre-suicidal,
masturbatory fantasy."

It's at this point that I realize my wife is brilliant,
and I'm a fucking idiot.

Jen proceeded to break the movie down as if she'd
been married to a better director than me for the last
three years, and suddenly, *Mulholland Drive* crystallized for me and rocketed up from shitsville to hitsville.
Thanks to my wife's explanation, I went from charging
David Lynch with one-trick laze to seeing him as the
true best director of the year—so much so that I
wanted to find out where Ron Howard lived, break
down his front door, grab the Oscar he'd just stolen,
and present it to the guy who really deserved it instead.

But, because I'm so fucking megalomaniacal and
self-centered, the whole affair started me thinking
about my life. At age twenty-three, I made a dinky,
dirty, amateurish black-and-white film about working
in a convenience store that Miramax—in what can only
be described as a drunken fit of generosity—picked up
for worldwide distribution. And for whatever reason,

over the course of the last nine years, I've been able to parlay that fledgling effort into four (going on five) more movies that I've directed, five other movies that I've produced in some capacity, including an Oscar nominee, four invites to the Cannes and Sundance film festivals, a heavily-trafficked website, a multi-million-dollar merchandising concern, a handful of awards, a side career writing comic books, numerous talk show appearances, an ill-fated TV show, gigs directing commercials, a monthly column in *Arena,* too many trips abroad, two beautiful homes, a stunning wife (who I met when she interviewed me for *USA Today),* an adorable child (who I met when she popped out of my wife), more money than I ever dreamed I'd see in this lifetime, and countless other blessings.

All of which begs the question . . .

Is my life one long, feverish, pre-suicidal masturbatory fantasy?

If it is, then please, God—don't let me cum.

Ever.

An Interview with Tom Cruise

HUMPHREY BOGART. Cary Grant. John Wayne. These are the movie legends of my youth—the giants whose names, synonymous with Hollywood-derived megastardom, lived on long after the men who bore them shuffled loose from the mortal coil. Like Zeus, Poseidon, and Neptune, they are dormant gods who have entered the pantheon of pop culture folklore, forever etched into the consciousness of even modern-day audiences who, like me, probably never saw many, if any, of their films.

Few actors working today can claim that level of

recognition while they're still *above* ground, let alone are guaranteed that kind of immortality once their box office sun has set and the universe wraps them for good. Few actors working today can be viewed as living history, as larger-than-life marvels who will still be remembered by generations of your descendants who've never even heard *your* name, let alone know what you did with your life. Time honors few men in such a fashion. So when you're offered a chance to talk to a living legend, you leap at it—if for no other reason than to be able to tell your grandchildren "I met him once."

But let's be honest—the real reason I'm interviewing this guy is pretty simple: this is the only chance I'll ever get to work with Tom Cruise.

Although when I enter the room to meet him, I realize perhaps I've underestimated myself.

"Silent Bob!" says the man who made lip-synching in your underwear de rigueur for anyone left alone in their parents' house, his arms outstretched, beckoning an embrace.

Suddenly, *Top Gun 2: Jay and Silent Bob Buzz Maverick* doesn't seem so far-fetched.

And as the mighty biceps of Cruise enfold me, I realize a) I'm not going to be able to write anything but a glowing piece about the guy, and b) I'm in love.

Cruise is perhaps the most beautiful man I've ever gazed upon: stunning bone structure, captivating eyes, perfect coif, killer smile, and not an ounce of fat on him. We're meeting to discuss his latest film, the Ed Zwick–directed epic Japanese period-piece, *The Last Samurai*. We're sitting in a dojo-like room high atop a Japanese hotel in downtown Los Angeles, complete with sliding paper doors and bound-feet geisha-like hostesses who serve us American substitutes for green tea (water and Diet Coke), then bow as they shuffle backwards, exiting the room. To complete the custom, neither of us are wearing shoes, affording me a look at the feet which hold aloft the box office's golden god. Even *they're* perfect.

But Cruise, pretty boy though he may be, has never been one to rely solely on sex as a weapon. His actor's arsenal is well-stocked beyond his locks and looks. The man can act. More than that, the man doesn't really even simply *act:* he inhabits the characters he plays in

such a fashion that you forget Joel Goodson is Charlie
Babbitt, who is also Lt. Daniel Kaffee, who is also Ron
Kovic, who is also Mitch McDeere, who is also Ethan
Hunt, who is also Jerry Maguire. He's been in twenty-
five movies since his debut in 1981's *Endless Love*, not
counting a cameo here or there (uncredited in *Young
Guns,* playing himself in *Goldmember)*. By his second
film, he distinguished himself as an actor to watch,
holding his own against old warhorses Tim Hutton and
Sean Penn in *Taps.* By his fifth film he was a bona fide
movie star, outrunning Guido the Killer Pimp in
Daddy's Porsche in the instant-classic *Risky Business.*

But it was his eighth film, the megahit *Top Gun,*
that firmly established Cruise as a movie icon with box
office clout. As Maverick, the headstrong pilot with a
penchant for buzzing the tower, T. C. powered the fifteen-
million-dollar jingoistic flag-waver to a sky-high $177
million in ticket sales (and mind you, those are 1986
dollars). Since then, he's worked with a who's who of
directorial heavyweights that any actor would give
their left nut or right ovary to lay claim to: Scorsese,
Stone, Levinson, Spielberg, Scott, Howard, Reiner,

Pollack, Jordan, DePalma, Woo, Crowe, and Kubrick. He's been nominated for a Best Actor Oscar twice, married as many times, and is the proud father of two.

But none of it may have come to pass, had he never left that Franciscan seminary.

"My parents had just gotten divorced, we didn't have any money. My mom was working three jobs," Cruise explains, poised on the edge of his chair. "There was always a side of me that was spiritual. And it was just a very complicated time. It was tough. My mother had moved from Canada to Kentucky, was raising four kids. I was searching for answers. What is life? What am I doing here? I felt that ever since I was a kid. When I was six, seven years old going, okay, what's this about? Is this it? This *can't be it!* My father went from Catholic to Episcopalian to atheist; Mother was a spiritual woman. I always had a sense that there was more to life. I believed that man had a soul, or was a soul. Or was a spiritual being, not just his body. I learned very early on that when, if you're dealing with problems, just looking at someone as a body doesn't work. You know? Doctors don't understand, neurologists don't understand chemical makeup. Even today you read none of these drugs work. We all know they don't work. Adderol, Ritalin, Prozac—you know, it's not *resolving the problem.* They're always looking at the *symptoms.* I had difficulties in school trying to pass, and I said, 'Okay, if I really crack down here I can do it.' [But] toward the last year, I didn't want to go to the graduation and they actually said if I don't go to graduation, you're kicked out. And I said okay. My mom was home, and I went down and told her I didn't want to go to graduation. She said 'How's everything going?' and I said 'It's fine, yeah.' I didn't tell her I'd just talked to Father Jeremy and he'd just kicked me out of the seminary!"

Cruise's affection for his mother is bottled-water clear. When he speaks about her, it's in the enthusiastically reverent tones usually reserved for best friends.

"My mother is an extraordinary woman. She's a woman who will literally go up to someone in a restaurant if they look sad and say, 'Do you want me to sing?' And she'll sing them a song to make them laugh. And it's not a show. It's just a sense of, you know, you have a choice. Your cup is half full, or it's half empty. And I believe my cup is half full. And there were times when I was an adventurous kid, I would, as soon as I could walk, I'd leave the house. And she'd ask, 'Where are you?' And 'What are you doing?' But she never held me back. I'd climb to the top of the trees and hang on the thin branches as the wind is blowing back and forth to see if I could hang on. And she never pulled me back and said, 'Oh god, you're going to die! Don't climb on that roof!'

"But she had some very simple, powerful things that carried me which is, you know, taking me as a little kid and putting me in front of the mirror and saying, 'Okay, how do you feel about this guy? Because the only one who's going to make you happy is you. And you have to be proud.' And I remember when I became a parent I turned around and I really started recognizing what she did for me."

Mental note: drag my kid in front of a mirror when I get home, in an effort to make a Junior Cruise.

"She still has an adventurous spirit. We went sky-diving together as a gift. She loved it! She'll fly in my P-51. This summer at Lake Powell we were water skiing.

She snow skis. She wants to play volleyball. She's just a person who wants to live life."

Aside from being one of the most exhausted mothers I've ever heard of, Mother Cruise has to qualify as Proudest Parent on the Planet. By now, the pride reserves must be running dangerously low, so over-accomplished is her baby boy.

"She feels a great [sense of] responsibility [for my success]. I'm sure you feel this as a father: there's nothing better in life than to teach someone something or to help them and be there and see them win. See them succeed. It's very gratifying. I'm not talking about self-congratulatory, I'm talking about a sense of that person is doing better [because of me] and that's a really good feeling. She feels that all the time.

"I realized early on even with all the traveling and I was always a new kid, that I can't depend upon others to define who I am. I want to *know* who I am, and so I was searching, I was looking. I was always looking, is this it? I mean, with my reading I tried many different kinds of reading programs, and I knew that I was not getting the comprehension. We don't get a manual with life. And the answers that I was getting weren't helping me. You know, blaming my parents, or blaming other people for my existence, didn't work for me. 'You are this way because of the chemical makeup, you are this way because your dad kicked your ass when you were a kid.' That doesn't help me with my life. I feel more bitter when I go down that road, it's not making me feel *better* about life."

The young Tom Cruise grew up in a house "with three sisters, father and a mother. We traveled around every year. Every year we moved into a different house.

"Father would move from job to job, parents got divorced so Mother wanted to move. We came back to Louisville, Kentucky. And then Mother remarried so we went to New Jersey for a year and a half, almost two years."

New Jersey? I knew there was something I liked about this guy.

"The four of us, me and the three girls, we traveled so much. Yes, there'd be fighting, but you know, we were a tight-knit group. We were best friends. Because wherever we went, we were the new kids. And we had the weird accents, we had the weird clothes. The four of us, because we were so close in age, we were going to the same schools together, during different times— especially Marion and I. Marion is a year older than me. And Leanne is a few years older than my little sister Tess. But no one could say anything about my sisters. *I* could say something about my sisters, but don't any- one ever, ever say anything. And it was the same with them. We protected each other."

But what about when he wasn't getting his sisters' backs? Surely li'l Tom Cruise was knee-deep in chicks! "During that time when I was about 13, 14, 15 years old, I had to work. I was either doing sports or having to work. When I lived in Kentucky, I'd go to the mall. I remember doing that kind of after I had a newspaper route, and we would go to Krispy Kreme on Sunday mornings, and we'd go to the Bartstown Mall with our extra cash when we got tips. And that was my mallrat period."

He used the term "mallrat." I swear I could marry this man.

Cruise has this power to make you feel like the sun is shining only on you when you're engaged in conver- sation with him. Some insist this is his Scientology training, but that kind of charm can't be imparted. I think it's a mixture of pure charisma, plain ol' nice-guy-ism, and a touch of Prom Queen Syndrome. This is, after all, the world's biggest movie star. Surely people find themselves too intimidated to talk to him. So like the prettiest girl in school, I'd wager he winds up standing off to the side by himself, more often than not, with people afraid to approach him to simply shoot the shit. This builds up a reservoir of attention that he affords anyone confident enough to chat him up like a normal person. He's attentive when he speaks to you. He listens carefully, gracefully sharing the floor. And if the constant mantra running through his mind is "I'm Tom Fucking Cruise!" he never lets on about it. He's as pleasant and chatty as a bartender on a slow night, happy to talk about any subject at all.

Like Scientology.

"I'm a Scientologist, been one for twenty years, and there are tools and things that I use in my life to help raise my kids so that they can be themselves. You know, educational tools that I wish I had when I was a kid. My kids, they can tell you at eight and ten how a four stroke engine works, and it's because they apply these tools in their life, and I apply these tools with them. And it's given them greater freedom and understanding and puts them in a position where they are more in control of their lives. And when you read the stuff in Scientology you kind of go, 'Well that makes sense.'

"Scientology has definitely helped me to be the kind of person that I know I am. And it doesn't matter how many millions I make or lose, I feel that way about life. And I've been able to be a better man. I realize my own responsibility, my own choices in my life, and my own integrity. And in this business that is tough. And life is tough. And I wouldn't be here today without that help, no way.

"When people apply it correctly and they use it, I mean, it's something . . . Someone doesn't apply it to you, you apply it to yourself. Someone says, 'Here's a tool, here's the key, does it start the car?' You take the key, put it in, it starts the car. And that's a beautiful thing. It's not about being Jewish, Catholic, Buddhist, Muslim. There's a reading study technology. You don't have to be a Scientologist to use study technology. It's secular. And it was intended that way. And that's what the thing is, it's not about saying you're this, so you can't be that. You have faith there? Good people who are Catholic, they still go in and do a purification, a detox that helps to cleanse the chemicals out of their body.

"I don't want people to tell me who I am. I don't want people to say, 'You know what I know?' I want to discover it for myself. You have kids. You say, *'You're being like this!'* It never works that way. They know who they are, and they want to discover it, and that's what I dig about [Scientology]. It's about being able to be more causative in your life. So when I study something, right now I know there's nothing that I can't learn."

There are a few things I'd like to learn myself, so I switch into fan-boy question mode.

K: You're one of the only actors who's worked with Sidney Pollack as both director and costar. Which one's better: Sidney Pollack actor or director?

T: Both great. He's riveting on screen, he's very specific. He started out as an actor and worked with

Meisner and I'm sure you know the whole history of how he became a director.

K: I don't.

T: He was an acting coach on one of Burt Lancaster's movies and Burt Lancaster said, "Who is this guy?" He started getting notes from Sidney, and he said, "You should be a director." He sent him over to direct television in Hollywood. And that was the beginning of Sidney Pollack's directing career.

   He's one of the good guys. He's really just a good man. He doesn't talk about that, how many people he's helped. He's generous and loyal. He's just . . . like straight sugar. I've got a lot of respect for him as a man. And you know, he came onto *Eyes Wide Shut* to shoot for about a week or two weeks, and ended up staying a couple of months! [laughing hysterically] But it was cool because he taught me how to cook.

K: You've directed once. You did an episode of *Fallen Angels* for HBO.

T: Yeah—for Sidney. I did that as a favor for Sidney. He said, "Direct this."

K: So you've gotten a taste for directing. Are you ever going to direct a feature?

T: I don't know, I've been offered things, and I enjoyed directing. It was fun. You're shooting 35 setups a day; I learned a lot. But as a producer and an actor it helped to do that. Really opened my eyes doing that, but I don't know. You know what it's like directing.

K: Sure. I mean, it's not like acting. When you're an actor, you can have two movies, three movies possibly come out in a year. You can get a lot more done as an actor than as a director. Directing requires clearing the desk. And I imagine it would be tough for you to clear the desk.

T: That's two years. You're talking two years. That's why I like producing. Because I like hanging out with directors and writers and I like working with them. And I am a junkie for the process. You know what it's like: you're making a movie, and you get your team together. And you guys are all going, and it's a mad rush and it's a real thrill when you're working on the script, or finding the story or finding a moment in a scene or something is clicking, or even when it's not clicking, how do we figure it out? And then the war stories and the adventure of making a picture, it's wonderful. But as a director? Me? Maybe one day I will, and I'm not saying that I won't, but I just don't have anything that I have to say. I would like to do it, but I don't feel *I must direct! I am a director, I must direct.* I like the relationship as an actor with the director. I enjoy it as much as the producer/director relationship. It's a fun relationship, that dynamic, trying to figure out, "What is it this guy wants? What am I looking for here?" You're supporting that vision and learning from it. And challenging each other. Because directors have different tastes when it comes to the performance. You look at Kubrick—his taste in performance is totally different than Sidney, what Sidney wanted, and the same with Barry Levinson, or, you know, Ed [Zwick], what he was looking for and the demands of that character, the demands of that story. I enjoy that process tremendously.

K: What's your process for reading a script? A script
lands on your desk, then what?

T: The first thing I do is I'm looking at the script as an
audience, and then I read it again as the actor. I just
experience the movie the first time. It takes me a
long time to read a script. I want to understand,
what is it the director is interested in? If it's a
writer/director, what is it they're looking to say? I'm
trying to grasp what they want, where they're
going, you know, where's this journey going to take
me? But I'm not very analytical about it, I'm just
experiencing it. The next time I go through, I go
through as the actor looking for the character.
Sometimes it takes months. I worked *Rain Man*
two years before we started shooting, [*The Last
Samurai*] almost a year before we started shooting.
Magnolia was a whole different process. A lot of
that was ad-libbed.

K: Most of your films have what I call the Cruise
Moment: the moment in which the whole perfor-
mance is crystallized, and I'm blown away. Now,
Magnolia is a film I've gone on record as not really

being much of a fan of, although I dug your performance. In that film, you're pretty amped up,
until the journalist starts revealing your past to you
in the interview, and you give her this cold stare
and utter:

T: "I'm quietly judging you."

K: A fantastic moment. The other moment that leaps
to mind is in one of my all-time favorites, a movie I
dearly love, *Jerry Maguire*—where you look at the
fish in the kid's room and say "It was a mission
statement..."

T: I could tell you both of those moments were
moments that each director talked to me about the
first time that I went through the script. It was like
the thing they really wanted—that line, and that
moment, you know? I mean, Cameron was like
"This moment—you gotta understand what this
means." He couldn't wait to shoot *that moment!*

K: Do you remember your first day on *Endless Love?*

T: I'll never forget it. First movie. I didn't know anything. Being there, in the schoolyard, it was the first

day and someone says "*I want you to go over and hit that mark.*"

I didn't know anything *about* marks. "A mark? Hit Mark? You know, you want me to go hit Mark? I'll hit Mark harder than anybody's ever hit this guy!"

I'd screen-tested and I did the monologue from *Does a Tiger Wear a Necktie?* I just got a call one day and I got this small role in this movie. So I remember I was living in New York, and I flew in to Chicago, I'd just turned 18. And I'd go in there and Brooke Shields was there, she was beautiful. And I kind of didn't know what I was doing. I didn't know about hitting the marks, the lines, and [snaps fingers] it was over. And I remember I went to a classroom and they wanted me to ad-lib something there and we did it and the scene never made it into the movie. And I just sat there on the set and I was like, "Who's doing what here?" The guy's coming up and I remember every person that came up to me I quietly said, "What do you do? What are you doing?"

K: When did you know it was going to be acting?

T: I went to so many different schools, I knew this is

what I wanted to do. I'm not going to go to college, I'd saved money and I was actually going to travel through Europe on a bicycle. And I was just going to take off by myself. And I ended up borrowing $900 from my mother and stepfather and said "I'm going to New York. I'm going to try this." And my mom was very supportive. Very supportive. But I knew that's what I wanted to do.

K: Do you remember much about *Taps?*

T: I remember hitchhiking to my mom's back in Jersey to get something to eat that weekend, after the audition. I had no money. And I used to hitchhike sometimes when I went back home so I could save money and I walked all over New York. And then they called and said I got the role. So I went to Valley Forge, Pennsylvania with [producer] Stanley Jaffe and Timothy Hutton and Sean Penn. And I realized it was a whole different world than I'd ever been in. Where you see the kind of talent that Penn had, and Hutton, and George C. Scott of course, I'd seen *Patton* many, many times. And Hutton I saw in *Ordinary People.*

I wasn't actually cast as David Shawn at the beginning. I had about three lines in the movie. And we had four weeks. They put us through military training. And in that four weeks having the opportunity to see Sean and Tim rehearse and [director] Harold Becker and Stanley create an environment for the young actors where we started doing workshops. And I learned more in those four weeks, I mean really. It was a whole different ball game in terms of what I thought. *This* is what I want to do. And at that time I remember I was training, and the guy who was cast as David Shawn, Harold Becker wasn't pleased with him. And after a couple of weeks they called me into the office and said, "Listen, we want you to play this character, David Shawn." And it was a supporting role. And I said, "Geez, no, I can't do that. I like this guy. I'm not going to take his role." And Harold said, "Well, kid, if you don't take his role, we're still going to fire him and we're going to go to New York and we're going to get someone else because he's not going to play it. I'm offering you an opportunity here. We think you're right for it. It's not your fault. It's just that we're going to do this." And we switched characters.

I had long hair, so I went into town into a military haircut shop. And I said, shave my hair off! So he shaved all my hair off, and I showed up back on the parade ground with a cap on, and I remember Harold saying, "Cruise! Come over here!" I said, "Yes sir." And he said, "What'cha got under there?" I pulled my hat off and I showed him and he said "Oh my God..." Harold wasn't pleased with me for about twelve hours.

K: So is that when you headed to Hollywood?

T: Well right after that I went with Paula Wagner as my agent [Paula Wagner is now Cruise's producing partner]. She was at CAA. I remember Sean invited me out to L.A. I remember he picked me up in a Firebird or a Camaro and I slept out in his guest house, and met Emilio Estevez. And we drove past Hoffman's house, Nicholson's house, and Brando's house. And we sat outside, and we're thinking maybe we should knock on the door now, maybe not.

K: Did you ever tell any of them that?

T: I told Hoffman. I don't know if I ever told Jack.

K: You've worked with a buddy of mine: Jason Lee.

T: Jason Lee is good, man! He's so talented. Huge! The work you guys did together! He's totally unique. And you're just watching him going, "Man I would never have thought to make that choice!" But it just comes out of him, you know? He's interesting, man. You just watch the guy. He's great to watch. I love working with him.

K: Before I came here, I told the folks at my website that I was going to interview you, and let them throw out a few questions. So here we go. "What's it like being one of the top actors for three decades, eighties, nineties, and two-thousands? And how do you plan on doing it for the next decades?"

T: That's a cool thing to say.

K: Well, it's true. *Three* separate decades, man.

T: I don't know. Just keep hammering. I remember when I was doing *Taps*, I would lose sleep. "They're firing guys on this movie, I could be gone tomorrow! They're shooting guys next to me! I shaved my head, he's pissed! What am I going to do!?" But

now? I don't know, I'm just going to keep doing
what I'm doing and make the movies, and seize the
opportunities of adventure and story. And keep
pushing myself to see what's next. And what's next?
You know, I'm doing this film *Collateral* with
Michael Mann.

K: "Do you ever want to write a screenplay?"

T: I've worked on story and I like working with writers.
But man, sitting down there, I don't know how you
guys do it. The *hours*. I enjoy the communication
with the writers, you know when you work on
scenes, and you talk about scenes, but that's a
whole different art form. I don't know if that's my
gig. I like ad-libbing and contributing and working
and challenging in that way, but sitting down and
writing a screenplay? I talk with Cameron. Cameron
just gets off on sitting down and writing. You're
probably the same way though, you know what I
mean? It's like you sit down and the monologue just
comes out and it has this dialogue that you just go,
"How did he think of that?" I don't know if I'm that
guy. I can take his stuff and understand his stuff and

contribute to it. Complement it. But I don't know if I'm that guy, that does that. Maybe one day. I've just never felt compelled to sit down and do it.

K: "Have you ever thought of doing any Broadway stage?"

T: You know, I might one day. I like going to the theatre, but there's really nothing worse than seeing boring theatre. You feel bad for the actors. I'm not saying never but I've never felt like I've got to go spend six months on stage. It'd be enjoyable to do it in a way where you get to start and stop every night. I've seen Hoffman do it, and I've seen Nic [Nicole Kidman]. But I've got kids, company, something. Maybe ten years from now I'd go do something like that. I like the immediacy. But I'm not burning.

K: "Has your mega-celebrity prevented you from making different types of films that perhaps you might be interested in taking? Like a backup or secondary role in a film that might have caught your eye without having the stigma of the 'next Tom Cruise film' attached to it?'

T: I felt that when I did *Magnolia.* But I don't feel that [being Tom Cruise] as a stigma at all. I feel that as a privilege. I feel that I have the opportunity to do things. I've never felt limited by it. I've never said, "Well, okay, I can't do this because..." But it's also a huge investment for me when I act in a movie. It's not, "Oh, I'm just gonna show up!" I mean, I could do something fun. I liked doing *Austin Powers*. I went in for four hours, had a laugh. I showed up in *Young Guns*. And then M*agnolia*. But I take a lot of pride in what I do, and when I do something, I can't just go, yeah, read the script, yeah, I'm going to go play. That would be me taking advantage of celebrity. I mean, any role that I commit to, it's an investment. It's an emotional, physical investment into that character. With *Magnolia* even though I only worked about a week and a half, ten days, I spent four months prepping that character.

These are great questions by the way, I gotta tell ya. This is cool.

K: "You've never done a flat-out comedy. *Risky Business* is funny, but not slapstick or farce. Will you ever do one?'

T: I love comedy. But when I look at guys like Jim
    Carrey, when you look at Robin Williams, Adam
    Sandler, Mike Myers—those guys are really funny.
    They're off the wall in terms of what they do. But I
    like comedy with drama. One of my favorite scenes
    in *Born on the Fourth of July* is where the two guys
    are arguing over who killed more babies.

K: That's some pretty dark comedy.

T: I remember the first time an audience saw *Rain
    Man,* they didn't know it was funny. They didn't
    think it was funny. There I am grabbing Hoffman by
    the back of his neck saying "Stop acting like a fuck-
    ing retard!" And I remember the audience was like,
    "Whoa!" It was really wild. They didn't quite get
    that it was okay to laugh in the rest of the film.

K: And last question. This one's my favorite. "What do
    you think Joel Goodson would be doing with his life
    today?"

T: [laughs; thinks] He went on to college and became
    one of those corporate guys that probably got
    trashed in the Internet fall.

And with that, I say my goodbyes and let Tom Cruise walk out of my life. I remember reading a quote from Renee Zellweger, who said something to the effect that, after *Jerry Maguire,* it took her months to get over Tom Cruise, so convincing was his performance. I was starting to feel a bit of separation anxiety myself as I took the elevator down to the front of the hotel and waited for my car.

And then it happened.

Cruise exits the building, heading for a waiting car. He's on his cell phone, earpiece in full effect. I offer him a wave, and he bee-lines toward me, removing the earpiece. He shakes my hand again, firmly, and says, "That was a really great interview, man. Thanks for that. It was a great way to end a long day of press."

He smiles, puts his earpiece back in, gets into his car, and drives off.

And suddenly, the sun's not shining on me anymore.

PART THREE

Lap Dance

HERE'S SOMETHING I've never told anyone else: I used to get off on pissing in a cup.

It was in the preteen era, when sexual awareness begins rearing its ugly, purple head. I'd hit the bathroom—usually when the house was empty—carrying a small juice glass that nobody in my family ever used (I hope), fill it, and stare at it for a few minutes. I don't know why, but I thought that was "hot."

Eventually, though, I needed to push the edge of the envelope. I discovered masturbation—which proved far more satisfying than pissing in a tumbler could ever be. And in time I lost the inhibition about masturbation that comes with Catholic Guilt. The realization that, in the Court of Self-Fondling, everyone's guilty freed me up to discuss the methods and frequency of "one-man-banding" with my friends. We spend many an hour debating all things masturbatory: which stroke book is better—the over-the-counter brands or the twenty-dollar, see-deep-in-the-brown-eye books you can pick up in Times Square; are two paper towels better than a sock as a mess-free catch-cloth; do you think about the present girlfriend or the ex—and if it's the present one, then why weren't you skipping the middleman and simply having sex with her? But there is one conundrum that—to this day—still plagues our jerk circle.

Why is it that whenever I got into a nudie booth, I could never jerk off?

For the sheltered few who don't know what a nudie booth is, I'll paint the filthy picture: you go into a small room, stick a token in a slot on the wall (evoking sex immediately) and a panel rises, revealing a Plexiglas window into a world of lust. On the other side, a woman—usually nude—sits on a bar stool and puts on a revealing show. Just how revealing depends on how many tokens you insert.

Every time I went to a nudie booth, I was hell-bent on jerking off. That's what it's all about. But the irony was that in a commercial setting designed specifically for masturbation, I didn't even lower my zipper. Every time, I picked up the phone receiver (used to communicate with the woman behind the glass, providing further emotional distance). I never conversed perversely, never detailed the insertions I longed for her to illustrate. Instead, I'd inevitably wind up having a ten-minute conversation with the woman about:

a) Why she chose this profession
b) What her net income is
c) If she's involved, and if she is
d) What her boyfriend or girlfriend or husband thinks
   about her job

Why was my fascination with trashy activities coupled with a crippling inability to join in? I knew it was all an escapist fantasy scenario, but the realization that I was role-playing deflated the luster, and I'd find myself conversing topically with a pube-shaven coed.

I can trace it back to the first time I ever patronized a strip club—back in '89, when I was nineteen. In Jersey, the ones that don't serve alcohol are called juice bars, and since there's no hooch on the premises, the strippers are allowed to get completely naked. My friend Bry and I sidled up to the bar, ordered our Yoo-Hoos, and took it all in with wide-eyed, laid-back enthusiasm. But it wasn't the girls that we found captivating: it was the men around us. They made strong, direct eye contact with the strippers and caressed their breasts as they slid a five or a ten into their cleavages. It was disturbing. These men were convinced that they could "have" these girls. You could see it in their eyes. They sincerely believed that—come night's end—they could bring the strippers home and act out what they were saying with their hardcore gazes. Bry and I left more depressed than anything else. We spent the car ride home berating the guys who bought into the whole scenario, puzzling over how anyone could be so misguided, and swearing that we'd never turn out to be the sorry individuals we'd just witnessed.

And then, years later, I took a trip to Toronto.

For those not in the know, our neighbors to the

north operate the finest strip clubs on the planet. Beautiful women, adorable accents, sanitary surroundings, and—unlike the Jersey all-nude strip clubs—beer on the premises. According to my hosts of that weekend, this was what made the White North great. And while taking in a show at the Brass Rail, Toronto's premiere peeler bar, those hosts offered to pay for a lap dance on my behalf. I'd never done it and, though I fought their charity at first, the offended glance the stripper shot me when I declined made me succumb.

So she took me by the hand and led me to a dimly lit room, where she directed me to an enclosed booth that housed a comfy armchair. As I sat, she proceeded to unsnap her threadbare excuse for an outfit, and tossed it to the side. The fact that she was totally nude jarred me—every lap dance I'd seen or heard about involved semi-dressed women. This was not the case in Canada, obviously.

The song began and she poured herself into my lap, and began grinding, as if we were a couple of teenagers in the precoital throes of passion. I started the conversation right about then.

"How long have you been doing this?"

"Hunhh?"

"I said, how long have you been doing this?"

"Four years here. I used to work in London, but I couldn't stand the commute."

"You stripped in London?"

"I was an emergency squad nurse during the day. Then I'd come here."

"You'd travel all the way from London to Toronto just to do this?"

"London, Canada."

"Oh."

And as the song concluded, she asked if I wanted to go again—ten bucks a song. I agreed, and we continued our conversation, this time with her leading.

"You look familiar. You're not from Toronto, are you?"

"I'm from Jersey."

"You look familiar."

"Ever hear of a movie called *Clerks*?"

I've never been above a shameless plug.

"Is that the one where there's a sign on a cash register that says 'If you're gonna steal something, tell us'?"

That's when I started to fall in love.

"Something like that. Have you seen it?"

"No, but I read an article about it. Are you in it?"

"More or less."

"That's cute."

And as she ground into me over the next forty-five minutes, and my wallet got considerably thinner, we got to know each other. She told me her name. Then she told me her real name (strippers usually go by stage names). She seemed incredulous when I told her my name was Smith, but I assured her it wasn't a ruse.

But it was the eye contact that got to me. She locked into mine and I drank deeply of hers. She flirted; I flirted back. And at the end of every song, she'd ask me if I wanted to go again, occasionally letting two or three songs go by without charging. From time to time, my hosts would cruise by to make sure I wasn't dead, and I'd introduce them to my lap-companion and then wave them away. And all the while, I slowly forgot what I'd so staunchly believed about buying into situations like this, scarcely aware that the manner in which I viewed the client/stripper relationship was about to be forever altered.

"Can I kiss you?" I asked.

"What?!"

"Can I kiss you?"

"We're . . . it's not allowed. I could get fired."

"Really?"

"Oh God, yes. The managers are strict about that."

"Sorry."

The irony of her being so chaste about a kiss while she pressed her bare crotch into my lap did not escape me. And after a beat or two, I guess it didn't escape her either.

She kissed me. On the lips. No tongue. Very intimately.

And with that, I was sold. She'd risked her job, even her safety for all she knew. The moment could not be ignored. Something that almost never happened in that dark room transpired between us.

But I was out of cash.

Fortunately, the place was also closing.

"Would you like to go ice skating?"

"What? When?"

"Tomorrow."

Long pause.

"Okay. But I have to work at five."

"How can I reach you?"

"I can't give out my number. If they see you writing it down, I'll get fired."

"Just tell me. I'll remember it."

She did, and the date was set for one the next day, after a phone call at noon.

The whole ride home I was razzed by my hosts, who registered abject shock at my loss of sensibility. They swore that the number she gave wasn't real and, instead of skating on the morrow, I'd wind up catching a flick with them. I shut them up by telling them that she had given me all my money back before leaving.

Of course, I was lying.

The next day at noon, I called. Then again at twelve-thirty. Then again at one. Then again at two.

And then I caught a flick with my hosts.

I felt like shit. I'd bought into it; I'd become one of the sorry bunch I shook my head at. How long would it be before I was jerking off in nudie booths now, or making strong eye contact with the dancers at the peeler bars, knowing in my heart that they *wanted* me?

I'd been duped. The moment I thought we'd shared was just so much smoke to hide the reality—she was in it for the money.

The next morning I caught a plane to Jersey. As I checked out of the hotel, the concierge gave me a message, dated the previous night at ten o'clock.

It was from her.

I threw it out.

I haven't been in a strip club or a nudie booth since.

Kevin Smith—writer/director of Clerks, Mallrats, *and the upcoming* Chasing Amy—*is the only man in America who cried when he saw* Showgirls . . . *and not from laughing so hard.*

Degrassi

I USED TO WORK AT THIS CONVENIENCE STORE, and on Sunday mornings the only thing that kept me from gutting the customers in a sleepy rage was *Degrassi Junior High*.

See, I had to make the papers on Sunday morning. And being one of the enlightened few who espouse the old adage "misery loves company," I made my good friend Jason Mewes ("Jay" to my "Silent Bob" in *Clerks*, *Mallrats*, and the upcoming *Chasing Amy*) help me. Together, we've dealt with more copies of newspapers than Hearst (although it's fair to assume he profited far more from it than Mewes and I). And we did it all while watching the *Degrassi* hour block on PBS—which might explain to the gentry of Leonardo, NJ, why they

237

so often had to return to the store for missing sections of the paper.

For those of you not familiar with the show... well, I just feel sorry for you. The precursor to the Stateside *Beverly Hills, 90210,* and far superior as well (sorry Shannen), it revolved around a high school in Toronto, where a mixed-bag group of ethnicities dealt with the trials, the triumphs, the passions, and the pits of teenage life.

You had characters like Joey Jeremiah—the guy who always wore a hat and got left back; Caitlin Ryan—the epileptic beauty queen whose road to hell was paved with good intentions; Snake—whose older jock brother turned out to be gay; Wheels—whose parents were killed by a drunk driver; Michelle—whose father didn't want her dating a black guy; and Spike—whose freshman-year pregnancy raised the eye of many a Canuck. The shows dealt with teen sex, child molestation, wet dreams, abortion, animal testing, divorce, braces, and bras—never in a condescending fashion, always intelligently. You'd be hard-pressed to find a more realistic show, or one more well-cast than *Degrassi*—especially on Sunday mornings.

Such a fan was I, that I named a character in my
first film after Caitlin. And in my second film, the character Shannen Doherty played can be seen wearing a
"Degrassi Junior High" jacket. Our recently completed
third film features as set-dec a framed bus ad from the
show's 1990 season, as well as a reference in dialogue.

Yes—I'm a member of the cult of Degrassi.

And I've often tried to figure out why. I know Jason
liked it because of all the teenage girls with pert breasts
and cute accents ("What are you talking *aboot*?" was
his favorite saying for some time), but for me, it was
more than that. I think it had something to do with
high school in general, a time that—until *Clerks* took
off—I assumed were the best years of my life. And the
show reflected that with every episode, calling to mind
an era when one's largest crises were wondering when
you were finally going to get to third with a girl, or the
possibility of a shitty grade in gym. I was reminded of
those better days every Sunday morning while in the
process of permanently staining my pigmentation with
newsprint, and fighting back the halitosis horde of pre-
noon customers.

And any program that helps one forget they're jockeying a register—even for an hour—has to be brilliant TV.

Kevin Smith is a writer/director who—upon coming into serious money—purchased the entire run of Degrassi from a scholastic video supplier. It was the best three grand he ever spent.

PART FOUR

Me, Walt, & the Garden State

EVEN THOUGH I'VE LIVED HERE my entire life (indeed, I now reside two blocks from the hospital which facilitated my emergence from Mom's nether regions), I only discovered New Jersey in late '88.

It was a transitional year for me—probably more so than the one that would follow in '94 (when I went from having a minimum-wage *job* to a maximum-wage *career*, thanks to luck, timing, and a potty-mouthed little piece of trash cinema called *Clerks*). I had just graduated high school (with no clue as to whether or not I'd follow it up with a stab at higher academia or what the Pythagorean theorem *really* was), my longtime girlfriend had dumped me (which meant I'd have to fend for myself as far as orgasms were concerned), and I had no circle of friends to speak of (having let most of them fall by the wayside in an effort to concentrate on the aforementioned girlfriend and orgasms). I had a job that was winding down at the town's recreation center (a position in a yearlong, state-funded latchkey kid program that had started the previous December), and a vague notion of becoming a writer. Short of that, there was nothing. I was a guy with no friends, no intimate companionship, no prospects. The future looked dark.

And then one day, I struck up a conversation with Walt Flanagan.

The guy in question—Walt Flanagan—was another rec employee I'd worked—more or less—side-by-side with over the last year. But short of a first-week two-minute exchange about his interest in the Devils and my sometime ability to secure tickets to games, we hadn't talked to one another. Ever. Can you imagine? I worked with this guy every damn day, and we never spoke to one another. There was no enmity or anything—in quintessential New Jersey fashion, it just came down to neither of us having much to say to one another.

I'd known of the dude vaguely from the early days of high school and only in the broadest of terms—he was an upperclassman with an eighties' metal mane. Walt ran with a crowd of denim- and leather-wearers who sported *Judas Priest* and *Slayer* album covers painted on their jackets (the mid-eighties were halcyon days for the metal movement). He wasn't as flamboyant as, say, Ed Hapstak (a friend's brother who was rumored to have been a devil-worshiping King in Satan's Service—a myth later debunked when we became friends and he confessed a deep fondness for Disney's *The Little Mermaid*), nor as approachably affable as, say, Bryan Johnson (the acerbic wit of the head-banging crowd, who'd been involved in one of those epic/tragic/masochistic high school romances since he was, like, nine), but one thing was clear about ol' Walt Flanagan regardless: he defined the quiet, seething aimlessness of the hard-rockin' high school set.

The conversation in question, the one that basically forever changed my life and brought me to where I am today (sitting before a word processor, trying to make a deadline for *New Jersey* magazine), was one that you'd imagine would be committed word for word to memory; one would suppose that I even have it inscribed somewhere on samite, custom-framed, and suitable for viewing, so important was the discussion.

Sadly, I don't.

I can't remember who said what to whom first (perhaps it began with a joke at the expense of the Amish, perhaps not), and I mark that as one of life's great ironies: so often, the details of what shapes us most in life are forgotten over the course of our day-to-days. If we knew how important a moment was going to be to us one day, I imagine we'd record it or preserve it better. Sure—we'll pay through the nose to have our weddings videotaped; but can we say the same thing about the first time we discovered masturbation, or the moment we realized that the true nature of the opposite sex was to lie and humiliate (and I'm not just talking about women here)? Usually not.

No—I can't recall what started the conversation between me and Walt Flanagan that day. But I do know that sooner or later, it came around to one very monumental topic—the one that made the stars and planets align, and fixed my destiny from that point forward.

"You collect comic books?" I asked incredulously.

"Yeah," Walt said, without a hint of shame.

"Get out of here."

"What's so hard to believe?"

"What kind of comic books? Metal ones?"

"Any kind. Batman."

"Batman?" I scoffed (remember that—at that time—the only mainstream awareness of Batman anyone had was the campy '60s television show). "I did a report on Batman once. For an English class."

"Get out of here."

"I did. I called it 'Capes, Clothes, and Panty Hose: A History of Batman.' Talked about this psychologist who attacked the comics because he said Batman and Robin were gay. Book was called *Seduction of the Innocent.*"

"Frederick Wertham."

"Yeah! That's the guy's name. I had stuff in there about Aunt Harriet, and how they added her character to remove the taint of two bachelor guys living together in a mansion."

Back then, when a guy spoke about Batman and

referenced a show-only character (like Aunt Harriet or Chief O'Hara), it was a clear sign that they were talking out their ass (it's easier to fake it now, thanks to the *Batman*-movie franchise). Walt seemed to lose interest in the conversation—clearly, I was out of my depth in discussing Batman. We fell back into silence. I figured that was that.

The next day, though, rather than allow me to wallow in my lack of Batman acumen, Walt presented me with a gift: a trade paperback of Frank Miller's revisionist take on Batman, *The Dark Knight Returns.* "Now *this* is Batman." He nodded. "Read it." I did, and it was an eye-popping, soul-burning, heart-racing meal which left me jonesing for more. If this was what comic books were these days, I wanted in—badly.

The question right about now should be: *What does all of this have to do with living in New Jersey?*

That day, Walt brought out the comic book fiend in me. And a comic book fiend has a habit to feed—a weekly one.

The following day, Walt (who had no license, even though he was years beyond the legal driving age) had me drive him to The Fantasy Zone, *the* comic book store in Red Bank (hell, in all of Monmouth County, for that matter). Rows and rows of books beckoned, and under Walt's tutelage, I answered their siren call. And we continued like that for a few weeks—hitting Red Bank for a weekly fix of comics.

But, as with any addiction, it began to not be enough.

We scoured comic periodicals for other stores—ones outside of Monmouth County. And I—as designated driver—clocked many miles trekking all over North and South Jersey, searching for that hidden gem of a shop—the one that housed that one last title we just *had* to find.

And along the way, we discovered this great state of ours—together. A couple of cats who—of their own accord—never really ventured out of their hometown of Highlands were suddenly finding themselves in Montclair, Bayville, Flemington, Barnegat Bay. And as we ventured up and down the parkway and turnpike, Walt spun truisms about New Jersey like an old timer who'd seen it all: from the day Molly Pitcher lived up to her name, to the riots that forever altered the nation's perception of Newark. They were truisms I still agree with to this day:

1) *Going south on the parkway is better than going north.* The reason being that there are more trees and shrubbery—both of which tend to obscure the fact that you're getting farther away from Highlands. The more north one went, the more apparent it was that we were miles from home—as Highlands didn't have any oil refineries that we knew of.

2) *The tolls are the work of people who don't appreciate comics.* Five tolls equaled one new comic—any fan of collecting would never have so many people waste so much money that could be going toward the latest issue of *Grimjack*.

3) *New Yorkers really don't know how to drive.* In fact, no out-of-staters know how to drive.

4) *The summer of medical waste washing up on our beaches was a good summer.* Sure—it was beyond disgusting and a blight that our beaches have yet to

live down; but it kept the damn "bennys" away. Fewer "bennys" meant less summer traffic, and less of a wait for the important things in life: movies, pizza delivery, and, of course, comics. The only thing better than medical waste hitting the beaches would be sharks (which would pose no threat to native New Jerseyans, as none of us go swimming here anyway).

5) *The state must have its finger on the pulse, some-how—they built an IKEA here.* Either that or we're just very European.

6) *Having "The Garden State" on license plates doesn't make nearly as much sense as, say, "The Exit-Happy State," or "No—we don't all have that accent."* Because it is and we don't.

7) *Danny DeVito had no right to name his production company "Jersey Films" if he wasn't going to base it here.* Be honest and call it "I Left Jersey Films," you traitor.

8) *The Joker hailed from New Jersey.* We could all walk with a bit more pride knowing that long before he maniacally uttered "Here's Johnny!" in *The Shining,*

Jack Nicholson was dealing with toll-booth fury too.

9) *We should've been Jersey musicians.* Bruce. Bon Jovi. Tons of broads. It seemed like a no-brainer, and often we cursed our parents for not putting a six-string in our hands instead of Weebles when we were waifs.

10) *No matter what anyone says about us (and Jersey has been the butt of many a joke), at least we aren't New York.* This was a thought that always came while doing ninety out of the Lincoln Tunnel.

People ask me why I love New Jersey so much, and why I set my flicks there. I can't say that I would've for certain, had Walt Flanagan not—in his own yeoman-like manner—opened up the Garden State to me—both geographically and philosophically. On our comiquests, he exposed the beauty and uniqueness that few see when they dismiss the state so casually (usually those friggin' New Yorkers). It was a lesson unintentionally taught, along with a more important one that I only fully realized once I began traveling outside the state:

that no matter where you go in the world, sooner or later it winds up looking like New Jersey... only with a few less thirty-five-cent tokens and beaches.

And all of that from a guy who actually liked Mötley Crüe.

Kevin Smith has written and directed three films (Clerks, Mallrats, and Chasing Amy—all set in New Jersey). He and Walt Flanagan still trek across the Garden State looking for comics—now for their own comic book store, Jay and Silent Bob's Secret Stash (the comic book store in Red Bank).

Preproduction

Dear Diary,

There's this boy in class that I'm just dreamy over.
He's got pretty blue eyes, brown hair, and a huge,
monster cock that barely fits up my...

Shit. Wrong diary. Lemme start over.

Ahem

Exclusively for you Poop-Shooters, starting today, I'm
going to irregularly (read: the columns are gonna be late,
folks; bet on it) chronicle the making of View Askew's
newest flick, *Jersey Girl*. I'm gonna sell you the inside dope
in nickel bags and eight balls, and if there's any juicy, Page

Six–worthy hot sex on the set between *you know who* and *you know who else,* I'm gonna detail it for you, position by nasty position (naturally, I'm talking about me and my longtime producer, Scott Mosier; *everyone* wants to know if we're really fucking or not). That's my promise to you, dear reader—an honest, inside look at the spit and glue that makes up this picture. And why am I doing this?

Because I make up for being cursed with a small dick by having a really big mouth.

So without further ado, let me give you a little skinny on the first few weeks of preproduction.

WEEK ONE

Before a flick goes into production, a new company is formed to protect the larger companies financing the picture (in this case, Miramax and View Askew) from lawsuits. In our highly litigious culture, that kind of protection is essential during the run of the show—because you never know when Affleck's gonna accidentally blow someone's head off while practicing his skeet-shooting between takes.

Clerks had no production company title other than View Askew, because a) we didn't know any better, and b) Affleck wasn't in that flick. But since other people have been giving us money, the formation of a new production company for every flick has been a standard ritual. For *Mallrats*, it was Unstable Molecules; for *Chasing Amy*, it was Too Askew; for *Dogma*, it was Plenary Indulgence; for *Clerks: The Cartoon,* it was Toon Askew; and for *Jay and Silent Bob,* it was Askews Me.

This time around, we've dubbed the production company New Askew—a not-so-clever reference to the fact that *Jersey Girl* will be the first flick we make that's *completely* unrelated to the other flicks we've made prior to this one. That means no Julie Dwyer references, no Rick Derris references, no *Star Wars* references, no *Jaws* references (okay—there *is* a *Jaws* reference in the new flick), and most of all, no Jay and Silent Bob. For some, that notion inspires collective cries of outrage; for others, collective sighs of relief. I, for the record, can be found somewhere between the two. It's tough to give up the ghost, especially when you love those characters as much as I do. But all good (or highly derivative) things must come to an end, so Jay and Bob go bye-bye, and New Askew steps up to the plate.

New Askew has set up shop in the City of Brotherly Love, Philadelphia (the irony of a movie entitled *Jersey Girl* being based in Pennsylvania is not lost on us), and boy, does this town live up to the moniker. I've never encountered a nicer bunch of folks populating a major metropolitan area. Fuck, these Philadelphians make the legendarily polite Canadians look like Angelenos by comparison. While only here a few weeks, we all feel so welcome that the lone way we could feel any more so would be if the city took down that old Rocky statue and put up a Jay and Silent Bob bronze monument in its place.

Is that too much to ask, really? I mean, Rocky is *so* played-out at this point. Then again, so are Jay and Silent Bob.

However, lack of statue notwithstanding, we like Philly and her peeps thus far. Shit, we'd *better* like it, because it wasn't easy getting *to* Philly. Miramax wanted us to shoot the new flick in Toronto, initially. And while Toronto is a lovely city, there's just nothing up there that remotely resembles the world we're trying to recreate, unless the world we were trying to recreate has a Tim Horton's Doughnuts on every corner, and a little maple leaf in all the logos on the 7-11 signs.

Oddly enough, Jersey itself wasn't really an option, based on how cost-prohibitive it would've been to shoot in Highlands (the shore town our new flick is largely set in). Highlands, unfortunately, falls outside the sixty-mile radius of the "Zone"—a nebulous union parameter outside of which the show is forced to put up and pay per diem to every crew member who has to travel to the set. Ultimately, this adds to the budget, and we can't afford to spend the money there, as whatever green *isn't* being spent on the *de rigueur* coke and whores has to be allocated for making Philly and the surrounding areas look more like New Jersey.

By basing the production in Philly, we can take advantage of the wonderful crew base that's been growing here, courtesy of M. Night Multi-Syllabic-Last-Name (the *Sixth Sense* guy), who, apparently, refuses to shoot anywhere but the Philadelphia area, and has made the Powers That Be enough bank to stand by the courage of his convictions. When a brother's never made a flick that's broken the thirty-million-dollar glass ceiling, he doesn't get to stomp his feet and say "We're shooting the whole fucking movie in the *real* Highlands." Well, he *can,* but he'll wind up basing out of Philly anyway. Money talks, and motherfuckin' Silent Bob walks.

Another beneficial aspect of Philly over Toronto is that we can simply cross the Ben Franklin bridge and actually shoot *in* the damn state the flick's named for. The nearby town of Paulsboro will be playing the role of Highlands for most of the show, when Highlands isn't able to play itself. For the purists (namely me), however, we've scheduled a few days of shooting in the *real* Highlands, as well as a few days in Manhattan— the city that also plays a crucial role in the flick.

But I'm not gonna lie: the *biggest* advantage to shooting in Philly is the cheesesteaks. The whole fucking flick can go straight to video for all I care, so long as I get to chow down on cheesesteaks for the next few months.

Speaking of straight-to-video, for those of you wondering "When the fuck are they gonna stop giving this cheesesteak eating motherfucker money to make his dopey stoner flicks, when they could be giving *me* all that cash to cinematically realize some of my awesome *Babylon 5* fan-fic?" I'd like to lay out some box scores, so you can handicap the likelihood of *JG* ever being a good picture, a successful picture, both, or neither.

Our start date (at press time) is August 19th.

Our wrap date is slated to be November 1st.

Jersey Girl is our sixth flick.

It's our fourth flick with Laura Greenlee, our intrepid line producer (the real brains behind the operation).

It's our fourth flick under the aegis of Miramax (*Clerks* doesn't count, because—while they distributed it—we made that on our own steam).

Unless we somehow piss off the Catholic League again, it'll be the fourth flick we've made that Miramax distributes (Miramax sold off theatrical distribution rights on *Dogma* to Lion's Gate, and the now-defunct Gramercy put out *Mallrats*).

It's our fifth flick with Ben-wa Affleck.

It's our third flick with George Carlin.

It's our first with Jennifer Lopez, Liv Tyler, and Raquel Castro (the tyke who plays the Jersey girl in question).

It's the first in which I won't be acting (if it can, indeed, be said that I've ever really "acted," outside of making wide eyes and shrugging on cue).

And, it's our third flick with a new director of photography.

THAT LAST POINT BEARS SOME EXPLAINING. Since Miramax is ever on a quest to improve the look of my flicks, we've, yet again, been asked to secure a different D.P. I keep telling Miramax Big Kahuna Harvey Weinstein "It's not the shooters, man; it's the director. You want better-looking flicks than what I've been giving you, you should hire a different *director*, not a different D.P.," but, alas, it's an argument that falls on deaf ears.

This pattern of the 'Max dictating our D.P.s started back when we were told that the gent who shot our first three flicks, our boy-wonder D.P., Dave Klein, was not going to be allowed to shoot *Dogma*. The bigger cast, Miramax argued, called for a bigger D.P. That time out, we landed Bob Yeoman, shooter of such flicks as *Drugstore Cowboy* and *Rushmore*. When *Jay and Silent*

Bob rolled around, Miramax once again asked us to switch D.P.s, which led us to Jamie Anderson (*The Gift, Small Soldiers*), who most agree shot our best-looking movie. That's why it was kind of shocking (and stressful) when Miramax again told us to get a *new* D.P. for *JG*. We kicked and screamed for two months, but when you don't hold the purse, you don't hold all the cards.

To be fair (and to avoid the inevitable phone call from Harvey in which he says "I'm pulling the plug on your bullshit movie, you gossipy fuck..."), lest they come off more poorly than they did when they opted to make *Kate and Leopold* (I think I hear the phone ringing now), Miramax has always done right by us, and this flick is no exception. They've given us Philly over Toronto (which cost them a couple bucks). They've ponied up for Affleck, Lopez, and Tyler (which cost them a lot more bucks). They're staking our largest budget to date (bucks upon bucks). The fact that they wouldn't bend on the shooter, while frustrating, wasn't something we could really hold against them; they just wanted what they felt was best for the flick.

So after two months of arguing for Jamie, we had to

cave and look for another D.P. The upshot to all this, however, is that when one door closed, another one opened. The D.P. we found is something of a legend, not to mention an Academy Award–winner. He's made a flick or two you might have heard of . . .

"Academy Award Winning Cinematographer Vilmos Zsigmond and Visually Challenged Director Kevin Smith."

Deliverance
Heaven's Gate
McCabe and Mrs. Miller
The Witches of Eastwick
Blow Ou
The Rose
The Deer Hunter
The Last Waltz
Close Encounters of the Third Kind

His name is Zsigmond. Vilmos Zsigmond.

So one of the world's greatest D.P.s is shooting one of the world's least visually inclined directors' new flick.

And thus begins the story of *Jersey Girl*.

Production

GUESS I COULD GET ALL HYPERBOLIC and
describe the production thus far in terms so incredibly glowing that the cynical and pessimistic reader will
swear it all reeks of spin control. But rather than subject you folks to that ...

All right, fuck it—I'm gonna subject you folks to that.

Jersey Girl is, hands-down, the best movie we've
ever made.

Granted, we're only in week two, but I feel comfortable going on the record with that confession. Now for
some of you, calling this flick our best probably isn't
saying much (as there are cats who feel we've never
done anything cinematically worthwhile). For others,

you'll never agree (the hardcore *Mallrats* fans won't find much to love about this flick). But for me, as my jaw drops watching the performances spark to life while we shoot, as I marvel at the dailies every night, and smile widely when Scott and I cut the scenes together over the weekends, that's the impression I'm getting. This flick certainly isn't the funniest film we've ever made (far from it), but it's already the most visually rich affair, with the most thoroughly realized characters I've ever had the pleasure of watching any of my casts commit to celluloid. As we come to the close of week two of our scheduled eleven weeks of shooting, for the first time in my career, I feel like a full-fledged filmmaker, as opposed to just a writer who directs his own stuff.

Rehearsals went incredibly well. We were scheduled for two full weeks, but by the end of day one it was clear that we could've started shooting the next day. In the midst of rehearsals, we took time out to head into Philly's famous Sigma Sound (where Bowie laid down tracks, many moons ago) to record a song for the big musical number in the flick.

Yes—I said big musical number. Where's GLAAD now, as I prepare to unabashedly unfurl and let fly my drama-fag flag by showcasing my adoration of show tunes?

When the rehearsal weeks came to a close, we did a pre-shoot day, which technically would be day one of the shoot, but it's classified as a camera test so as to not be reflected in the budget as part of principal photography, all while giving us a jump on the schedule. Essentially, the pre-shoot day is a dress rehearsal for the shoot itself, as this preliminary day affords the cast and crew a hint of what it's going to be like to work together.

The most startling aspect of the pre-shoot day for me was that we did two beautiful crane shots. What's weird about this is that we've done maybe two crane shots total in all of our previous movies combined (all right—really it's about five or six), and there we were, not even the first day of the schedule, and already Vilmos was making with the cranes.

The crane we tow around with us, created by our key grip, Dicky Deats, is an amazing and storied piece of equipment, which won its maker an Academy Award for Technical Achievement back in '83. Dubbed "The

Little Big Crane," it lives on our grip truck and was constructed in fairly easy-to-transport pieces (but, mind you—this is coming from a guy who just watches grips move shit around; so for all I know, those pieces are, in reality, heavy as fuck) that can be assembled rather quickly at any location. In other words, we've got this crane that's so pliable, we could take it up the elevator to the fiftieth floor of a skyscraper (which we've already done), or throw it together to make a simple shot of a dude walking from his car to his front door look far more impressive than the act really is.

There's one Little Big Crane shot in particular—a crane-into-a-closeup of Raquel—that's so gorgeous and powerful, it changes the shape of the script altogether. After watching it a few times, I opted to drop two smaller scenes that precede it, so as to make that shot the first moment we see Raquel's character in the movie. Granted, the cut-before-we-shot-'em scenes weren't that long (maybe a half page each), but still—me cutting dialogue out in favor of visuals? Letting pictures tell a story instead of words? That's akin to Hitler saying "The Jews ain't so bad. Let's turn the Reich over to 'em."

This is just one of the benefits of working with guys who've been making films since I was in Huggies—the vast repository of know-how and experience they offer. There's nary a problem that either Vilmos, Dicky, or Bill O'Leary (Roger Deakin's gaffer—or chief lighting technician—who Vilmos secured for this flick) can't suss out. I tell ya, we're so technically adept this time around, I feel like Spielberg—only, y'know... without the desire to replace the guns in my previous flicks with walkie-talkies.

Speaking of which, we wanted to use a clip from *Jaws* in *Jersey Girl*—the shot of Quint being eaten by the shark. It was the focus of a short scene between George Carlin's character Bart and his granddaughter (the titular *Jersey Girl*) in which he used the movie to instruct the child in the perils of swimming at the beach. The word came back from Amblin that Spielberg didn't want to license scenes featuring the shark, based on the primitive special effects in the flick (i.e., the shark looks fake).

When we chose another scene that didn't showcase Bruce himself (we opted for the death of the raft-riding Kintner boy—the one whose remains the mayor didn't want to see spill out all over the dock), the word came back that Spielberg didn't want to license the use of any scenes in *Jaws* that reminded people how scary the movie was.

The long and short of this story, kids?

I smell a digitally manipulated rerelease of *Jaws* in which the shark menaces Amity with a walkie-talkie.

DAY ONE—THE BIG SCENE

Up first, my wife made out with Jason Biggs, as Affleck looked on. Shortly after that, we started shooting the actual scene.

We started with a humorous, light scene, set at the Christmas party thrown annually by the music division of Mandel/Kirschner, the publicity firm that Ollie Trinke (Ben's character) works for. The bit serves as an introduction to Biggsy's character, Arthur Brickman— Ollie's right-hand man. Jen (my Jen, not Affleck's Jen) plays Susan, Arthur's office paramour, and the two of them turned in ace performances that acted as a sort of palate-cleanser for the moment that follows: the meeting of Ollie Trinke and Gertrude Steiney (Jen Lopez).

If you're ever shooting a movie about two people falling in love, I can't urge you strongly enough to cast a pair of people who are actually falling in love. The chemistry between Ben and Jen is so palpable, you could almost bottle it and sell it as an aphrodisiac. Take after take, we watched Ben and Jen (who we couldn't have cast as love-at-first-sighters at a better time in their lives) flirt through a rapid-fire-dialogue dance of movie meet-cute. But this wasn't just art imitating life; somehow in the midst of all that smolder, they managed to provide us with a pair of performances that reminded this little black duck why he's always worshipped at the Altar of Affleck, and is now currently constructing a Lopez Basilica as we speak. Honestly, the performances they gave were nothing short of spellbinding.

Take after take, Jen offered up a myriad of options—so much so, that when the time comes, it's a tough scene to cut. Every time we rolled, while delivering the same scripted lines, Jen provided something new, delicious, and real to choose from. I almost want to include three or four different versions of the same scene in the flick, just so the audience can see what we're seeing on the set. Even those familiar with how good she was in *Out of Sight* will be taken aback by how wonderful a performance Jen's giving in our little love story. And for the curious (or for those who believe what they read in the tabloids), Jen's not only a really sweet person who's easy to love (partly because she's very genuine, partly because of how very smitten she is with a guy I adore and think the world of), she's also the finest actress I've ever worked with to date.

But Bender's no slouch either—far from it. The man's turning in what is, for my money, his finest hour yet—which is saying a lot, as I've always felt his *Chasing Amy* and *Good Will Hunting* performances would never be beat. But not only has he beat 'em, he's bludgeoned the shit out of them and left 'em for dead atop the body of already strong work he's accrued since he first trod the boards for us as the guy who liked to fuck girls in an uncomfortable place, way back in the day. Along with the charming, smart, witty work that defines all of his performances, Affleck's turned in some really moving stuff thus far as well. If his "I love you—and not in a friendly way…" speech in *Amy* brought tears to your eyes, bring a whole box of tissues when you go to see this flick, because Ben's got a scene with the kid that'll just flat-out break your heart—even if you hate children.

All the while, Vilmos has been rolling two cameras simultaneously, capturing different sizes of the same setups. It's a time-saving method of shooting coverage, but it also means that by day's end, we've easily shot 15,000 feet of film. But footage-burning be damned, this is beautiful stuff. Vilmos' moody, sexy lighting of our trusty production designer Robert "Ratface" Holtzman and art director Elise Viola's gorgeous Manhattan office, and slow-moving camera crawls that lead to dazzling, killer close-ups make this the best-looking scene in any View Askew movie ever (big ups also go out to Diane Lederman, who fleshed out Ollie's world with her office décor, and Buster Pile, who built the set on the Naval Yard soundstage in our adopted city of Philadelphia).

By the end of week two we'd shot Ollie and Gertie's post-introduction dinner; an intense and somewhat sad scene involving Ben and Biggs; Ollie and Gertie's first fight (of sorts); one of the three crowds in front of which Ben's gotta deliver speeches; a more-dramatic-this-time-around George Carlin as Ollie's dad, Bart; the ever-genius Stephen Root and equally genius Mike Star as Bart's friends Greenie and Block; and stellar little newcomer Raquel Castro as the Jersey Girl in question. All of the stuff is dynamite.

BUT THE WEEK-TWO CAPPER was a 6-P.M.-to-6-A.M. shoot of the flick's opening scene, the actual Christmas party. Staged at Top of the Tower (on the fiftieth floor of a tall-ass building on Arch Street), this is the scene that introduces Ollie as he offers up a five-minute toast to his employees that concludes with an awkwardly war-bled and impeccably danced rendition of a classic eighties old-school rap tune. Remember Spender's moves from "It's Your Birthday" in *Amy*? This blows that out of the water. Affleck clearly missed his calling as a

Solid Gold Dancer. Christ on the Cross, if he didn't knock that scene out of the park!

My thanks go out to the tireless crowd that provided massive energy in the room for twelve hours, giving Spender something to work off of. Like the crowd in their sister scene from the Town Hall shoot the week before, these cats gave a tremendous collective performance, as good and lively by the last take as they were on the first.

I WISH I HAD DISH TO WRITE ABOUT—like how shit's falling apart, or who's fucking with our movie at the moment. But the truth is, it's blowjobs all around, as things couldn't be going more smoothly—which may make for a boring column, but sure makes for a great movie.

Post

YOU'LL HAVE TO EXCUSE THE DELAY in what was planned to be a weekly column—like my desire to ever weigh under two hundred, it was a pipe dream, at best. Trying to juggle too many balls will do that to you. Trying to juggle said balls while they're still attached to random tranny hookers you picked up on Santa Monica in the backseat of your family truckster behind the Dumpster of a Carl's Jr. is also not suggested, lest you be accused of "going Hollywood" and "selling out." But, oh... that sweet, forbidden tranny fruit...

ahem

All marital and societal deviancy aside, I'm bi-zack in this bi-zotch, and here's the latest beats to the rhyme...

THE MOVIE'S DONE. Shoot went incredibly well. Vilmos shot a gorgeous movie that nobody's going to believe I had anything to do with. The moment I got back to L.A., I locked myself in an editing room and haven't emerged since.

Until now.

Last night, I came to the bottom of the "Footage To Be Cut" bin in our Avid, and found there was no more movie left. With the exception of one scene we shoot on January 8, we're ostensibly done with the first pass. Didn't want to time it out yet, but I'm betting it's between 2:15 and 2:30. My latest mantra is "If *Jerry Maguire* can work at 2:18, we can work at 2:18..." but that might just be the high (and laze) of wrapping up a first cut talking. We'll see. Regardless, the movie can now be watched end-to-end, without me stopping every few scenes to explain to the viewer what happens next (now I only have to stop once).

As for the film—well, I'll say this: I fucking love it. I do. I really adore it—more so than anything we've ever done before. Outside of marrying Schwalbach and being too lazy to rip open a prophylactic that apparently had Harley's name written all over it (though not necessarily in that order), it's the best thing I've ever done. That's not to say it's for everybody; in fact, a good number of the folks who've loved our previous flicks will probably abandon us after seeing that *Jersey Girl* is nothing like them (not even *Amy*), if they even see it at all. Anybody who incorporates "Snootchie Bootchies!" into their Internet postings or daily conversations might wanna wait for the *Clerks* cartoon flick (which— take this as a promise or a threat—is next for us) and skip this one. I'll save you the time of having to post this on our Web board and let you know that I understand you feel I'm a "pussy," a "sellout," "I've lost it" (whatever "it" was), and I "eat cock." You're not going to change my mind about the flick; I just love it too much.

But lest it get hyped to disappointment, that's all I'm going to say about *Jersey Girl* right now.

whistles

Uh-oh...

Standard Smith inability... to keep... word or deadline... kicking in...

Must... gush... some... more...

AAAAARRRRRRGGGGGHHHHHHH!!!!

OKAY, A WORD OR TWO MORE ON THE SUBJECT.

Ben's so good in this movie, it makes me sick sometimes. You know how there are some roles actors seem just *born* to play (like Robert Shaw in *Jaws* or Barry Bostwick in *Megaforce*)? That applies here. Ben is the Barry Bostwick of the *Megaforce* that is *Jersey Girl*. Make of that what you will.

But how 'bout the folks I didn't get to talk about in the two previous columns, because we either hadn't worked with them yet, or they hadn't shot their killer scenes?

Liv Tyler. She's in the running, alongside Lopez, for best actress I've ever worked with. In fact, it's probably a toss-up at this point. To have one amazing female lead in a movie is a mitzvah of some sort (and I'm not even Yiddish, mind you) but to have two? I must have used up whatever good karma I had coming to me. And if that's the case, I'd say the universe is square with me, so far as I'm concerned (you hear that, Lord? I'm finally letting you off the hook for the small-dick thing).

Liv (or Sport-Fuck, as I call her) is that rare breed of actor who can do every line in the script without changing a word, and still craft a better character than was written. Maya worked fine on the page, but Sport-Fuck breathed life into her in such a way that, as I'm cutting her scenes, I'm not editing Liv's stuff, I'm cutting *Maya*. It's all about inflection and character—Sport-Fuck inflected herself to the most believable performance I've ever shot. She may be a horrible speller, but fuck if she isn't an insanely great actress. If you don't fall in love with her in this movie (and I'm including you in on this equation, ladies), then you're a robot, and your primary directive is to go rip a heart out of someone's chest and solder it into yours (for the curious mandroids out there, your secondary objective is to make sure Skynet doesn't go apeshit and wipe out humanity; I've got a lot of shit to do, and I don't wanna have to take time out of my busy schedule to defend me and mine against cold, unforgiving steel; take a page out of Rosie's book and vacuum a rug or something, maybe take Astro for a walk, but try to cool it on the mutilating of human flesh... particularly mine).

Master George Carlin. Anyone looking for Rufus (from *Bill and Neo's Excellent Adventure*) or Cardinal Glick (from that religious picture with the rubber poop monster in it) or even Barbra Streisand's gay neighbor pal (from *Prince of Nick Nolte Getting Boned Up The Ass Against His Will*) is going to find a hard time locating him in this picture. Carlin pulled out all the stops and gave us a Bart that only facially resembles George. At the risk of sounding like an ass who has no business saying this—as Carlin is a god and the smartest man on the planet, whose intellect I'll never have even five percent of—I'm *proud* of the man. I knew he could do it; it's why I wrote the part for him in the first place. But I didn't know he'd do it so well and touchingly. Don't let the "I wanna see shit blowing up and bodies falling out of the sky!" fool you, folks; Carlin's all heart—and that's never been more on display for an audience than in this picture.

Jason Biggs. I'll forgo the standard pie-fucking jokes and cut right to the chase: he's fantastic in this flick (and in *The Graduate* on Broadway, which he's no longer in, but still—it's worth mentioning). Biggsy's always funny (so much so that it landed him the lead in the next Woody Allen flick), but here, he shows off his dramatic chops as well. His Arthur runs the gamut from awkward amateur to confident professional, and you buy it every step of the way. I love this fellow Jersey boy. Look for him in more of our stuff, if he'll come back.

Stephen Root and Mike Starr are just flat-out funny, not to mention patient and just about the sweetest guys you'll ever meet. I'm not going to say they're the older, not-so-wiser Jay and Silent Bob of this flick, because I'm sure someone else will. If you ever need sublime, pitch-perfect character work done, these are your men.

Betty Aberlin deserves to work more than she does, as she's an underrated comedienne with tremendous instincts. She's woefully underutilized in this business, but we're aiming to fix that.

L'il Raquel Castro. She had to lift shit far heavier than any seven-year-old should have to, and she did it in spades. Gertie was never designed to be one of those movie-cute kids who utters precocious little bon mots and bats eyelashes; she was designed to be a *real* seven-year-old kid. And that's exactly what Raquel gave us. She's adorable, but not gratingly so, and I can't thank her enough for that. She's the quiet little heart of our film, upon whose very small shoulders the whole movie rides, and I can safely say that she handles that task like a pro. Expect big things from this little package.

And lastly, there's Slopez. I've gushed so much about her in the previous columns that all I'll say here is she finished as strongly as she started. We couldn't have found a better Gertrude. However, I will add this: I don't think I've ever cast an actor who's engendered as much ire and bile as Jen does—and it's all unfounded. She's too sweet and too hard-working to warrant shit like this being dropped in my e-mail (reprinted in its entirety, with name withheld) . . .

Kevin—

I am sending this letter to you, since you are a friend of Ben's. As a fan, I'm wondering if those who are close to him are unable to see a change in 'style' with him? I have never seen Ben wear the 'pimp style' jewelry that he is now adorning. I have seen this type of jewelry on Sean 'Puffy,' 'P. Diddy' Combs. More recently, I've seen it on Cris Judd. Since there is only one person connected to these three guys—Ben, Cris Judd and Puffy, I wonder who's influence this is?! It is also interesting and troubling to hear/see Ben out on so many shopping trips. Apparently, 'Jenny from the block's love does cost a thing!' Obviously, this is something that Ben is unable to see, now that he is wearing his rose-colored glasses. Ben once said about when he's in love that he has the tendency to be 'swept away.' 'Swept away' may actually be a good term and soon his bank account will be 'swept away' too, by the way he's going through the money with this materialistic user. As an outsider, you don't have to be a real genius to see what type of a person she is. Ben deserves much better than her. He is clearly being taken advantage of. What woman in her

position, when she has one of the most decent, gentle-
manly and handsomest guys around, would actually be
comfortable accepting incredibly expensive jewelry
from him? If I were in her shoes, having Ben Affleck as
my boyfriend would be all that I would need! I would
not trot him out everywhere, where people could see us,
using my relationship with him to generate talk and free
publicity. I have an enormous amount of respect for
him and it's heartbreaking to see him with someone
with immoral values. Someone that uses whatever guy-
of-the-moment she's involved with for something or
another. I hope that those who 'claim' to care about
him and those who say they are his 'friend' will prove
that they do care and that they are his friend, and not
sit back being a kiss ass with someone who uses men in
more than one way and doesn't take her marriages seriously. I hope that someone will have the balls to pull
him aside and encourage him to not rush into anything
with someone who's last two marriages didn't even last
a year! Eventually, J.HO will break his heart and in just
knowing that, it's heartbreaking. His fans don't want to
see him hurt and we don't want to see him rush into a

marriage with someone who obviously doesn't take her marital vows seriously and lies to God when reciting those vows.

Whatever you saw between them on the set of your movie, doesn't mean that it's 'true love running both ways.' On her part, it's lust and the fact that she's got a 'sugar daddy,' who'll do anything/buy anything for her because he's blinded by love. How heartbreaking that is!

I mean, who the fuck spends this much time dwelling on the affairs of people they've never met. Good God... But it didn't end there. Here's the rest.

Speaking of the movie, please note that Ben Affleck fans will refrain from all movies that feature him and J. Ho (AKA: Jennifer Lopez). Ben fans have no interest and are disgusted when it comes to movies that feature them.

"I am the Borax. I speak for Ben's fans."

BTW, when this 'relationship' breaks up, if Ben would

like to get involved with a girl who would respect him, not use her relationship with him for publicity or want publicity, and not need any material things-especially flashy in-your-face jewelry, who would consider Ben 'the only diamond" that she would need, let him know that she's in AZ and that my love don't cost a thing. Ok?

How genius is that? No agenda there, not at all. Fucking people can be crazy when they've got too much free time and an apparent lack of interest in their own lives. Someone cancel that girl's subscription to *US Weekly* and *People*, but quick.

And while we're in the mailbag, here's another e-mail I got, regarding the two previous *Jersey Girl* columns (again, reprinted in its entirety with name withheld) . . .

I need to ask you a questions about this update you have posted on your site: Are you kidding me with this sun-shine up the ass shit? I mean, I appreciate the fine sen-timent about how the cast is getting along and how breathtaking it must be to see love blossom between

"Bender" and "JLo," but Jesus, your column reads like a 10th grade love letter.

Fuck. I was going for at *least* 11th grade…

If you insist on being flowery, couldn't you at least try to sound a little less sophomoric

Man, I hope that pun was intended…

(pun intended)?

Phew!

If you won't, then I understand, but I think I'm gonna stop reading the column

You do that, and you'll miss seeing your condescension and bitterness in lights.

because I don't think I can take the obvious PR and promo anymore.

You know, not every kind sentiment is PR or promo. In fact, PR and promo are normally saved for around the time the movie's being promoted, not almost a year in advance.

But, hey—you're the shepherd, Will.

You are watched because of your wit, don't forget that.

Snappy Answer #1: See! I *knew* I was being watched! And people called me paranoid!

Snappy Answer #2: I thought I was watched simply because people couldn't see around my girth.

That being said, I think that you are a great talent and wish you the best of luck on your upcoming piece.

You had me at "That being said."

I am not a film maker or a director,

What a coincidence! Neither am I!

> just an actress who does a little law school on the side.
> Fondest Regards,

Quick! Send me your head shot and resume, and I'll cast you and pen 10th-grade-level sunshine-up-the-ass shit about you too!

On matters unrelated to *Jersey Girl* ...

Columbia/Tristar's *An Evening with Kevin Smith* DVD hits shelves next week. Two discs, between three and four hours of a fat guy sweating a lot and answering questions. If you're remotely into my shit, it's right up your alley. If you're not into my shit at all ... well then, what the fuck are you doing reading this tenth-grade-level, sunshine-up-the-ass shit for?

My involvement with *Scary Movie 3*. Here's the story: After the Wayans brothers took what was supposed to be *Scary Movie 3* elsewhere, Bob Weinstein called and asked if I'd look at the Dimension draft of the latest *Scary Movie* when they were done with it, and maybe add a joke here or there. I asked him who was writing it, and he said he hadn't assigned it yet. So I suggested a guy I knew was perfect for the gig: Poop Shoot's own Brian Lynch. Bob met with Brian, and brought him on as one of the writers, along with David Zucker and Pat Profft. For this, I was offered an exec producer credit. Somehow, the trades translated this as me cowriting. If *maybe* doing a polish on a script that will be far funnier than anything I can think up is considered cowriting, then I guess I'm a cowriter. However, with these three funny guys involved, chances are, I'll have nothing to add but the sound of my laughter (*with,* mind you; not at).

Spider-Man/Black Cat: The Evil That Men Do. I got bogged down with production, but rest assured, the last two issues are coming.

Daredevil/Bullseye: The Target. Some folks have bitched about the September 11th content of the book and how dated they felt it was (Good Lord, how quickly some people forget...). In my defense I'll say this: the script was written *last* December, a bit closer to the actual tragedy. But regardless, as a guy who saw those Towers almost every day for thirty years or so, their absence—not to mention the loss of lives and the horror of the act responsible for both—is something that will affect me forever. Maybe if you never lived in the tri-state area, September 11th doesn't have as much resonance, and you were able to go back to business as usual; but for New Yorkers and those of us who grew up in the shadow of the City, life still hasn't gone back to normal, and probably never will. I live on the other side of the country now, and it still haunts me. My apologies if those feelings, expressed through a character native to New York, got in the way of your desire to simply see a guy in tights beat the shit out of another guy in tights. You might want to skip the rest of the series.

The *Daredevil* movie. I saw it. It's great. Mark and Co. nailed the tone of the character/book. If you're a fan of the comics/character, you'll dig this flick.

The *Jen Saves Ben* game. Some folks have asked about when this is going to be available. Sorry—it was a wrap gift for just Bennifer. The guys at Powerhouse Animation (the ones behind that *Heroes* short with Cap and DD as Dante and Randal) created it, and did a great job.

There is, however, another game; two, actually.

If you're at Jay and Silent Bob's Secret Stash, you can check them out. There's one called *Jay and Silent Bob Save the Stash,* and another one called *Dogma 2: Electric Boogaloo.* They're pretty sweet, and if you ask Walter really nicely, he'll probably let you play them for free.

The Next Flick. Now that we're wrapped on *Jersey Girl,* I keep getting this "What're you doing next?" shit. Aside from the *Clerks* cartoon movie (which, once I'm done writing, is out of my hands and into the hands of the directors/animators), truth is, I'm not sure. There are a few options (*Fletch Won*—but only if they let Lee play Fletch; this sci-fi thing I've been toying with; and a pair of comic-book flicks: one that's very close to my heart and one that would be completely out of left field) but I've yet to figure it out. For the first time in the nearly ten years we've been doing this, I find myself at the end of one movie, not knowing what the next one will be. No complaints, mind you; it's actually kind of nice. But weird. Maybe it's time for a vacation finally.

PART SIX

Defender of the Faith

WHEN I WAS A KID, much to my chagrin, my grandmother watched *The Young and the Restless* every afternoon. This was a problem for me, as the campy, live-action *Batman*—my prepubescent *raison d'etre*—aired at the same bat-time on a different bat-channel. And try as I might, I could never boo-hoo my Grams into switching stations.

The older I got, the more fervently I'd rail against her soap—not so much in an effort to get her to spin the dial to *Batman,* but more to convince her on a purely critical level how insipid the show was. And Grams, God bless her, would always simply shrug, smile at me knowingly, and go back to enjoying the adventures of Nicky and Victor. Sure, I might've had a point in all my caviling; but she liked what she liked, and no amount of bellyaching was going to make her turn her back on what she called her "stories."

This summer, *Episode Two: Attack of the Clones* was met with a more churlish response from the critical community (both off- and online) than Richard Gere's plea for peace and understanding of other cultures at this year's Academy Awards. With the exception of *Time*'s young-at-heart Richard Corliss, most critics sharpened their light sabers and carved poor (theoretically, not financially) George Lucas a new one, as if he were a Taun-Taun and they were trying to save a Wampa-ravaged Luke Skywalker from the freezing winds of Hoth in *The Empire Strikes Back*. To use a less fan-boyish analogy, the Powers That Be beat the shit out of *Episode Two* like the movie had fucked their girl- or boyfriends behind their backs.

What were they all expecting that had them feeling so let down? I'll allow that in terms of predictability, *Episode Two* (and *Episode One*) will always make *Titanic* seem like a veritable whodunit. We all *know* the Empire's going to rise and eventually fall at the hands of Indiana Jones, the dude from *Corvette Summer,* the chick who wrote *Postcards from the Edge,* and an army of teddy bears. We all *know* that the Jedi will be hunted to extinction, with the exception of Alec Guinness. We all *know* that Yoda lives through the Clone Wars and matures into a Muppet. There's little to no mystery left in the *Star Wars* prequels, with the exception of seeing exactly *how* the space-shit winds up hitting the space-fan. And that should be enough to get even a casual fan into the theater.

Taken on those terms, I was enthusiastically *not* disappointed by *Attack of the Clones.* Shit, I loved it. Why?

Because I love a car-wreck.

That's what the new *Star Wars* flicks are to me: a stunning, tragic car-wreck. And I don't mean that in the pejorative sense, like this round of flicks is "sterile" as so many of the critics seemed to feel. You can throw a rock and hit a naysayer happy to pontificate about how Lucas has lost his humanity, citing the last two installments of the *Star Wars* saga as guilty of being more digitally manipulated than a free-spirited eighth-grade girl's breasts by her over-sexed boyfriend, but I'm not one of those cats. I'm digging the new installments for what they've *become*—the tragedy du Darth: the slow fall of Anakin Skywalker into the greasy clutches of the Sith.

And that little melodrama has never been more on-display than in *Clones.* Here, we're presented with the adolescent Anakin—the boy who'll later torture his own daughter (unwittingly, to be fair) and cut his other kid's hand off (rather wittingly). From the get-go, Lucas captures my limited imagination with one simple proposition.

Darth Vader was once a teenager.

How pedestrian, yet how profound! Evil's gotta start somewhere, right? Why not show *why* Johnny can't read—or, in this case, play well with others and stop using the Force to choke underlings who don't live up to his expectations? And from the hit-and-miss origin of *Phantom Menace's* take on baby Anakin as the galactic Hitler in short pants, *Clones* ups the ante by presenting us with the heart of darkness right where everyone's always known it lies: in the passions of a volatile high-schooler.

From the get-go, Anakin is portrayed as a kid who thinks he knows more than he does and insists on proving to everybody that he's as good as them, if not better. I went to high school with this guy. Granted, he didn't grow up to carbon-freeze anybody (in truth, I believe he works at a Shell station now), but had he been given a light saber and taught how to pull the Jedi Mind Trick on folks, he might've. Anakin in *Clones* is a twelfth grader with a license and parents who want him home by eight: he's a disaster waiting to happen. Who else but a tortured teen leaps out of a sky-speeder to capture a bounty hunter who's talked smack about his girl (or, in the case of *Clones,* set loose killer centipedes in her bedroom)? With little to no concern for his own well-being, based largely on his assumption that he's immortal (that worst of teenage attributes) young Skywalker forces Zam Wessel's craft (how sad is it that I'm thirty-one and I know the name of a character who's never really identified and appears only fleetingly in the film?) to crash-land in a densely populated city, and then pursues her (it) into a bar ... only to watch his mentor, Obi Wan Kenobi, make the final collar. And how does the Force-ful whelp wrap it all up with the wide-eyed cantina bystanders? He tosses them a condescending "This is Jedi business." The *balls* on this kid!

Fatherless, this rebel without a cause (or *Imperial* without a cause, technically) is shown to trust in the quietly power-mad Palpatine—the dad he never had, who fills his head with notions such as "I see you becoming the greatest of all Jedi." I knew guys in high school whose fathers would fill their heads full of this kind of bullshit too, along the order of "If someone gives you lip, you kick their ass." It's easy enough to take an impressionable youngster and turn him into a school bully, but the relationship of the would-be Emperor and his protégé is even more perverse, considering this is a kid who can telekinetically spin fruit in midair and Mind Trick a rampaging intergalactic rhino into playing Trigger to his Roy Rogers. Beating up freshmen for looking at you funny in the hallways is one thing; destroying a planet because you're looking for the stolen Death Star plans is something else.

And never mind the wacked-out paternal issues,

Anakin's relationship with his mother makes Oedipus'
seem healthy by comparison. And like the lunchroom
loudmouth who makes one mother joke too many, the
Tusken Raiders reap what they sow when Anakin
unleashes hell on a whole tribe of them for battering
Shmi. What teenage boy *wouldn't* slaughter the men,
women, and baby Sand People if he found his mother
dead in one of their huts? That's the origin of Darth
Vader right there: the guy who went apeshit when he lost
his Mom. Never mind that he'd been too busy galaxy-
trotting for nine years to even so much as send her a
Hallmark on Midi-Chloridian-Mother's Day; that's his
mom they fucked with, and they're all going to pay.
There's something bittersweet about the fall of Darth
Vader now, that hadn't existed before *Clones:* had his
mother simply died of old age, the guy might never have
developed that extreme case of asthma he seems to suffer from in *Star Wars, Empire,* and *Return of the Jedi.*

Which leads to the most haunting moment of
Clones for me: when Anakin breaks down to his puppy
love, Amidala, and confesses that he butchered that
no-good bunch of sand-eating bandage-wearers with

his high-tech Zippo. This scene really resonated with me, because Amidala wears this expression that very quietly says "Holy Christ...I'm in love with a human bomb." The sad, hopeless look on her face upon learning of his murder spree brought to mind that moment in *Jedi,* when Luke asked Leia if she remembered what her (and his) mother was like. Leia (in what may be Carrie Fisher's finest hour in the original trilogy) reminisced that her mother always seemed sad. Here, nearly twenty years later, we get to *see* what Leia was talking about.

And that's what worked best for me about the Anakin arc in *Clones:* the doomed love affair of Anakin and Amidala. Most of the critics dismissed this as the flick's most ham-fistedly handled aspect, but I thought it played out tragically and beautifully. High marks to both Hayden Christensen and Natalie Portman, because I completely *bought* their relationship. He wants her desperately without really even knowing *why,* as do *all* teenage boys when they find who they assume is their one-true in high school. And even though she *knows* this guy is poison, she can't help but fall for him—the little slave boy who grew up to be a conflicted, impetuous hate tank who insists everyone's giving him a raw deal. In high school, the really hot chicks *always* went for the massive fuck-ups, and eventually wound up married to them. But this marriage doesn't simply end in small town affairs and divorce; this marriage ends with the girl scattering her kids across the galaxy to save them from their father, who by that point is more machine than man.

The only thing that could've made *Clones* more enjoyable for me would've been if I was actually *in* it. (C'mon, Obi-George—isn't there room in the next and final *Star Wars* flick for a portly Stormtrooper who smokes too much?) And as I sat there watching that beautiful fucking car wreck, fully aware of the attacks *Attack* was suffering at the hands of the critical Empire outside that darkened theater, I finally knew how my Grams felt when I'd slam *The Young and the Restless.* Now *I'm* the one offering up the knowing smile— because I *love* that Lucas is still dicking around in a galaxy far, far away, and I never want it to end. The *Star Wars* saga is *my* soaps, and no amount of bi-otching disguised as film dissertation is going to get me to turn my back on my "stories."

Unless, of course, there's a new *Batman* flick out at the same time.

PART SEVEN

Years ago, the British magazine *The Face* asked me to
pen a humorous look at comic book conventions.
Apparently, my idea of humor and theirs (spelled
humour in the U.K.) didn't quite match up, as they
refused to print it. This is the first time that discarded
piece is seeing ink.

    Arena forever. *The Face* never.

Comix!

WHILE RECENTLY IN THE U.K., a journalist inquired of me whether or not American comic book conventions were anything like I'd portrayed them in *Chasing Amy*. He explained that there weren't many comi-cons in Great Britain, and what little he knew of the phenomenon and its attendees was from the dribs and drabs he'd read about in the American press and the representations we'd assayed at the head and tail of the flick. His take on the shows and the entire comic book subculture—while filled with stereotypes so clichéd that it made so-called computer nerds seem positively metropolitan—was nothing new: comic book people are geeky, dweeby, sexless onanists with no sense of the distaff and poor excuses for lives;

Trekkies without the requisite hard-on for Shatner.

Now, as a self-proclaimed defender of the faith, one would imagine that I'd leapt over the desk at the rube and tore him a new asshole—Wolvie-berzerker style. Instead, I merely smiled and shrugged. "What can I say? It's all true."

But it isn't.

See, I can be frank with you people because this is a British publication (granted, he was a British journalist, but one can never be too careful with journos—they're loose-lipped). I can come clean without fear of blowing the decades-old, carefully manufactured beard that comics fans have crafted in an effort to keep attention from our sundry agendas, because I know it'll never reach American shores (the land of comi-cons).

With that in mind, I've granted *The Face* permission to reprint some passages from the journal I kept during my recent visit to the ComiCon International in San Diego—the world's largest annual comic book convention. All I ask, gentle reader, is that you keep your mouth shut about it around any Americans, as the average comics enthusiast would like nothing more than to keep up the current status quo for the general public: the belief that comic collecting is for nerds. If this info got out, we'd have to deal with a lot more traffic in an already crowded "hobby," and if one thing about comic-freaks is clear, it's that we hate change (and bent covers).

DAY ONE:

Just arrived, and already I've scored some killer China White for the weekend. The lobby of the hotel looked like a damn brothel, as most of the guys were painting the tonsils of the hardcore comic bitches (those whores can't get enough of a guy who can tell you exactly what's been going on in the *X-Men* books for the last ten years).

After blowing a few lines with a dealer who hooked me up with some early bondage nudes of that *X-Files* chick, Scott (my producer) and I hit the Con floor. Inside, you could smell the debauchery like perfume on silk: while haggling for lower prices on *Deadpool* back issues, fans were negotiating for turns at unloading their DNA into the "floor-whores"—the chicks who paid admission to the

Con not to buy books, but to slam the dealers (notorious for being hard-bodied, well-hung beefcakes).

I sat in on a panel called "Grooming the Beard—How to Deal with the Curious Fan," and picked up a few more tips on dissuading jackoffs with a casual interest in the field from poking their noses in our good thing. A panelist (a dealer from Sacramento) told a story of a speculator who—after seeing a fluff piece about it on the news—came into his store to pick up twenty copies of the *Superman* issue in which the Man of Steel's suit was changed from the traditional red, blue, and yellow to a more powder-puff azure (another effort to put off would-be fans by besmirching their memories of the Chris Reeve film—a movie that brought so many fly-by-night fans to the field that we had to lay low with our shadowy antics until *Superman III*, when Richard Pryor effectively killed the franchise). It seemed the panelist was spotted by the fan in his back room with a couple of local councilwomen, playing strip–*Magic: The Gathering*, and snorting Diesel off their breasts. The dealer related how he had no other choice than to ice the bastard right there, lest word get out to the real world. I'd have been sobered, but mid-story, the woman in the seat beside me had slipped her hand down my shorts and began yanking the wank while rubbing herself off. We'd climaxed upon hearing of the fatality—another pseudo-fan bites the dust.

I wrapped up the day trading some Golden Age books for some newer stuff, looking for a quick turnover back at my own comic book store at home. I had the dealer throw in some Percocets to make it an even trade, and we split a 'lude to seal the deal. Dazed, I was sidetracked on my way back to the room by a sorority chapter from Omaha who ushered me into their *Spider-Man* hot-tub orgy, where me and Scott shot a lot of "web," if you catch my drift (my "wall-crawler" was deader than Gwen Stacy after that free-for-all).

All in all, a good start to the show.

DAY TWO:

I got snagged by a local news crew outside the Con, and—still hung over—I had to feed them the usual bullshit about being a "superhero dweeb" and how the crowd was made up of "primarily fourteen-year-old Bat-freaks." With a condescending chuckle, they wished me luck on my "treasure-hunting."

I spent the first half of the day in a six-chick/three-guy daisy-chain session, hoping to weasel out of this one buxom blonde a trio of low-numbered *Witchblades* I saw she had. I had to spend a little extra time yawning into her nether regions, but—lockjaw aside—it paid off. She gave me the books, and the number of her and her roommate, offering to let me watch them strap-on screw one another the next time I was in New York. Like I'll really call.

I picked up a few Image *Ascension* Convention Specials for a pretty good price, and then spent the rest of the day watching comics legend Stan Lee perform his annual Excelsior Multi-Bang—the centerpiece at every Con, when Stan mounts an all-nude porn opera: an unclad stage production of a classic *X-Men* issue, which always closes with the Man burying it deep inside twenty of the finest lookalikes the Con has to offer (you haven't seen anything until you've seen the comics legend tit-bang "Storm"). As usual, the audience went through the complimentary Ecstasy faster than the Con anticipated, and a few folks had to settle for rim-and-suck jobs from other attendees (both male and female; it was "in" to be bi this year).

I went back to my room with a couple of women who were hardcore Martian Manhunter fans. Turned out they worked in the Justice Department, and we toked on this killer Jamaican lambswool they'd confiscated from a case back in Washington. While Scott did the dog with the one, I engaged in some slow tantric sex with the other, all the while discussing whether or not Morrison's current run on *JLA* surpassed the stuff he did on *Doom Patrol*. I got her number before she left, but I doubt I'll call her.

DAY THREE:

The Con is always slow on Sunday, as that's the day the media does their floor coverage, and we have to take it easy. But while they were covering the auto-graph-signing booths of Lou Ferrigno (TV's *Hulk*) and Jeremy Bulloch (the guy who played Boba Fett in *Empire* and *Jedi*), the *real* autograph signing was going on in the no-press-access south ballroom. Willis showed up, as did Arnie and Mel. They did two hours of glad-handing and tripping with the fans, and then excused themselves to partake of the fruits of their labor—a no-holes-spared triple penetration with a hottie dressed up like *Wonder Woman*. The guys lucked out with orifices, but the cutie threw me a bone and grabbed my and Scott's pieces for a five-on free-for-all. Mid-coitus, me and Arnie talked about the hoax of *Batman and Robin*, and how happy we were with the B.O. returns and reviews.

That night, Warner Brothers screened the *real Batman and Robin* flick (directed by Jim Cameron, with a script by David Mamet). It kicked ass—especially since the crippling of Batgirl was right out of Alan Moore's *Killing Joke*. After the flick, the Warner execs toasted the demise of the "public" *Batman* franchise, as now the mainstream would lose any interest in comics-related flicks—thus keeping prying eyes away from our secret club. As an added treat, the floor show turned out to be a dildo act featuring none other than Uma and Alicia themselves.

While complimenting her on how deeply she could accept a fourteen-inch "Black Manta," Alicia and I got to talking about how good the latest *Preacher* storyline was, and how we couldn't wait until Garth Ennis crossed over into flicks. Something sparked between us—one of those show-only moments— and we went back to her room for some...

Well, I promised her I wouldn't say (suffice to say she slept on her stomach for the remainder of the evening).

And that marked the end of another year of hidden

debauchery; another year of testes-spraining sex marathons; another great Con.

We'd succeeded once more at perpetrating the great hoax for the mainstream that keeps comic-collecting such a fantastic hobby: that we're sexless dweebs. And in the end, it always befuddles me that they've never been able to figure it out and unmask our charade. I mean, without the sex, drugs, and occasional good deal on a pricey book, why else would grown men be into comic books?

Some folks just never see the forest for the trees.

P.S.—Before I left her spent in the sheets, Alicia handed me an absolutely naughty Polaroid of herself from our seven-hour "cram" session. On the back, she'd written her phone number, but in all honesty, I doubt I'll call her.—KS

Kevin Smith is the writer/director of Clerks, Mallrats,
and the just-released Chasing Amy. *He's sad to report
that—with the exception of the good deal on the
Ascension Convention Specials—none of the above is
true . . . not even remotely.*